SLAVE CAPTAIN

The Career of James Irving
in the
Liverpool Slave Trade

Edited with an Introduction

by

Suzanne Schwarz

bRIDGE
books

Wrexham, Clwyd

Slave Captain – the Career of James Irving in the Liverpool Slave Trade
© 1995 Suzanne Schwarz

ISBN 1-872424-42-2

Published in Wales by
BRIDGE BOOKS
61 Park Avenue
Wrexham, Clwyd
LL12 7AW

CIP Data for this book is available
from the British Library

Front cover illustration by courtesy of
the Board of Trustees of the
National Museums and Galleries on Merseyside

Printed and bound by
MFP, Stretford, Manchester

Contents

Editorial Conventions

Letters have been arranged in date order and, for the purposes of this text, have been numbered consecutively.

Footnotes are used in the letters and journal to explain terms, to identify individuals and to highlight other primary sources which provide relevant information. The notes are contained at the end of each section.

Original spelling has been retained, although words have been separated or joined according to modern usage.

The spelling of names is retained as in the original text.

Abbreviated signatures have not been expanded.

All abbreviations (other than names) have been extended where there is no doubt of their original meaning.

Editorial insertions are enclosed in square brackets.

[...]	illegible or missing word
[?]	uncertain transcription
[deleted]	deleted word which is not legible
~~word struck through~~	deleted but legible

Abbreviations

D.A.C.	Dumfries Archive Centre
H.L.R.O.	House of Lords Record Office
L.C.R.O.	Liverpool City Record Office
L.R.O.	Lancashire Record Office
M.M.M.A.	Merseyside Maritime Museum Archives
P.R.O.	Public Record Office
E.E.H.	*Explorations in Economic History*
J.I.H.	*Journal of Interdisciplinary History*
J.A.H.	*Journal of African History*
H.A.	*History in Africa*
T.H.S.L.C.	*Transactions of the Historic Society of Lancashire and Cheshire*

Preface

In the eighteenth century several hundred men spent part of their maritime career as captains of British ships that transported probably more than two million Africans to a life of forced labour in the plantations of the West Indies and America. Yet few personal accounts written by slave ship captains are known to have survived. The recent discovery, therefore, of the personal papers of James Irving, a Liverpool slave ship captain of the late eighteenth century, is of tremendous significance.

Irving's case is particularly informative. His successful career was interrupted when he was shipwrecked off the coast of Morocco, captured and sold into slavery and this newly discovered evidence reveals his emotional and psychological response to the period that he spent in captivity in North Africa. The efforts made by Captain Irving's family and friends to secure his release and the role played by the British Government and consular officials in Morocco, reveal a great deal that is familiar in light of modern day hostage negotiations. All the people active on Irving's behalf assumed that he was entitled to his freedom and that he should be reunited as soon as possible with his wife and family.

Letters written and received by Irving, together with a copy of his journal describing his period in captivity, were deposited anonymously in the Lancashire Record Office in 1977 and have lain unnoticed for sixteen years. This is surprising as even the brief catalogue entry manages to convey the intriguing nature of his story:

> correspondence of James Irving of Liverpool, mariner and slave trader, with copy journal ... when shipwrecked on Barbary coast, 1786-1809.

The process of reconstructing James Irving's career in the slave trade and his own period of enslavement has seemed, at times, rather like chasing a dead man. As one might expect, relevant sources have come to light in a number of different record offices in England and Scotland and each has suggested new directions of research. More unexpectedly, a visit to Langholm in Scotland, James Irving's birthplace, led to a meeting with a distant kinsman who owns letters written by the captain's younger cousin and namesake (hereafter referred to as James Irving II). As James Irving II sailed on three slave voyages with his older and more experienced cousin, and was also captured and enslaved off the coast of Morocco, his letters provide additional insight into their reversal of fortune.

The newly opened gallery in the Merseyside Maritime Museum which charts the history of the transatlantic slave trade, indicates the abhorrence of slavery in the modern western world. It is important to recognise that James Irving was just one of many British individuals who actively participated in, and profited from the trade in 'black cattle', to use a phrase taken from one of his letters.

At one level, Irving's case does contain a fascinating story and the author has deliberately emphasised the powerful narrative. The introduction is subdivided to allow readers to select those parts of the narrative in which they are particularly interested. Should readers wish to follow the story in Irving's own words, the journal is reproduced in Section II and most of the surviving letters relating to his case are contained in Section III.

At another level though, Irving's experiences illustrate many issues and themes which are part of the on-going academic debate on slavery (see Section I). Irving was, after all, employed by Peter Baker and John Dawson, a leading British slaving firm. Early in his career he served as a surgeon on the *Princess Royal*, the largest ship in the fleet of Baker and Dawson, which transported slaves from Africa to the Spanish colonies of America and the West Indies under the terms of legal contracts or 'asientos' with the Spanish government. It was probably Captain William Sherwood, acknowledged as one of the leading captains in the Liverpool slave trade, who recommended Irving for promotion to captain.

Discussion of Captain Irving's career can contribute little to the 'numbers game', a phrase used to describe the recent scholarly attempts to quantify the dimensions of the slave trade. The value of this newly discovered archive lies rather in what it reveals of the character of a man whose family life and future involved the continuance of the Atlantic slave trade.

Acknowledgements

I would like to thank my former colleague Gareth Williams, Dr. Michael Power and Professor Paul Hair for the encouragement and advice which they have generously given. I have benefited considerably from their expertise and ideas, and this manuscript has been improved by their detailed comments and suggestions. All remaining errors of fact and interpretation are, of course, my own.

I am grateful for the assistance which I have received from the staff of the Lancashire Record Office, the Dumfries Archive Centre, the House of Lords Record Office, the John Rylands University Library of Manchester, the Liverpool City Record Office, the Merseyside Maritime Museum, the Public Record Office, the Royal College of Surgeons of Edinburgh, the Royal College of Surgeons of England, the Royal Commission on Historical Manuscripts and the Scottish Record Office.

I would like to thank the County Archivist at the Lancashire Record Office for permission to include transcripts of Irving's copy journal and correspondence. A letter from James M. Matra to William Wyndham Grenville, included as letter 13 in the text, is Crown copyright and has been reproduced with the permission of the Controller of Her Majesty's Stationery Office (P.R.O., FO 52/8, 105-6). Two letters written by Captain Irving whilst in captivity, letters 10 and 11 in the text, are in the custody of the Public Record Office and have been included with their permission (P.R.O., FO 52/9, 115-117). I am grateful to the Liverpool Libraries and Information Service for permission to include a copy of the 1785 map of Liverpool and a transcript of a letter written by Captain William Sherwood (L.C.R.O., 387 MD 28). I would also like to thank Mr. A. Tibbles, Curator of Maritime History at the Merseyside Maritime Museum, for giving permission to use a copy of William Jackson's painting as the cover illustration. The painting of a slave ship is currently displayed in the Transatlantic Slavery Gallery at the Merseyside Maritime Museum.

Thanks are also due to David Irving for his help and hospitality, and for giving permission to include transcripts of three letters written by Captain Irving's younger cousin and namesake.

My special thanks go to Simon who has shared my enthusiasm and encouraged my interest throughout.

SECTION I: Introduction

1. Sources.

This discussion of James Irving's life and career is based largely on a collection of documents that has recently come to light in the Lancashire Record Office. This archive, held at reference DDX 1126, includes a copy of a journal written by James Irving which vividly reconstructs his shipwreck and period in captivity. The main part of the collection comprises Irving's correspondence spanning a period of five years. These letters reveal aspects of Irving's career in the slave trade as well as his period of enslavement in Morocco and the area now known as the Spanish Sahara. The correspondence is only partial though, as none of the letters written by his wife Mary, are included amongst these papers. This may suggest that Mary Irving, née Tunstall, was responsible for the form of this collection, choosing after her husband's death to preserve only those documents which recorded aspects of his life.

As these documents were only deposited in the Lancashire Record Office in 1977, it is likely that they were passed down through the family. Eight letters written in the early nineteenth century contain some important clues about James Irving's descendants, although the person who decided to give these rare documents to the Lancashire Record Office about twenty years ago remains anonymous. It is possible that they have retained James Irving's original journal. The document contained in the Lancashire Record Office is a copy written in a hard-backed, lined exercise book which probably dates from the early to mid-twentieth century. The person who transcribed this volume of some 10,000 words is not identified and the style of writing, although twentieth century in appearance, offers no precise clues to the date at which the transcription was made.[1]

As the account of his period in slavery is so colourful and compelling, I initially had some reservations about the authenticity of the copy journal. Yet there is no apparent motivation for anyone to fabricate the account which, until now, has remained unpublished. Not only are the details in the journal supported by many of the eighteenth century letters in the collection in the Lancashire Record Office, but many other sources confirm as well as expand upon the account in the journal. The most impressive find of supporting evidence was amongst Foreign Office papers in the Public Record Office. Contemporary copies of Captain Irving's letters are enclosed amongst the correspondence of James M. Matra, Consul General to Morocco between 1787 and 1805. Moreover, Matra's regular reports to Whitehall provide detailed accounts of the negotiations on behalf of Irving and his crew.[2] The one surviving letter written by Captain William Sherwood in the Liverpool City Record Office is a plea to unnamed individuals to assist in Irving's release.[3] Still more impressive was the discovery of letters written by James Irving's younger cousin and namesake, which lend further support to the account of events contained in Irving's journal and letters.[4] Captain Irving's family background can also be traced in the faded graveyard inscriptions in the neglected, overgrown churchyard of Langholm parish church.

I suspect that Irving's original journal still survives in private ownership. He may have written more than one as a way of informing family and friends of his experiences. In a letter written to his wife, Mary, on board the *Ellen* in 1791, following his return from Morocco, he expressed his hope that 'Mr. Smith has received my narrative' (Letter 39). His uncle, living in London, may have been the recipient of one volume, whereas the copy in the Lancashire Record Office suggests that the original from which it was transcribed was 'wrote by Mr. Irving for his much loved brother-in-law, George Dalston Tunstall'.[5]

Finding the original journal will complete the trail, and draw this chase of a dead man to a close. The introduction which follows though, is an attempt to reconstruct Irving's life and career by drawing together the strands of his story contained in a wide range of documentary sources.

2. Early Career in the Liverpool Slave Trade

James Irving, the son of an innkeeper from the Scottish border town of Langholm, built his career on the prodigious slave trade of late eighteenth century Liverpool.[1] As a ship's surgeon and then as a captain, he participated in the movement of slaves from West Africa to the Americas. This Atlantic trade, in which France, Portugal and Holland were Britain's chief competitors, accounted for the forced migration of some six million Africans in the eighteenth century alone.[2] In the last two decades of the century, a period broadly corresponding with Irving's career in Liverpool, it has been estimated that 1.5 million slaves were transported from the west coast of Africa. Of these men, women and children, perhaps as much as one-half were carried in British ships.[3]

A majority of British ships set sail from the port of Liverpool, which has been described by one historian as 'the premier slave-trading city of Europe in the eighteenth century'.[4] In 1789, a year when Irving achieved his first command, 61 ships sailed from Liverpool to purchase slaves in Africa for re-sale in the West Indies and America. Compared to a joint total of 33 slave ship clearances from Bristol and London, the leading ports in the early eighteenth century, Liverpool's dominance of the so-called 'triangular trade' was clear.[5] This pre-eminence was still more apparent in the final decade of the century as over three-quarters of the British slave clearances were from Liverpool (1002 of 1294).[6]

The part that James Irving played in the 'African diaspora', a term used to describe this forced migration of Africans and their dispersal in the New World, was comparatively small. During his career he was involved in a number of voyages accounting for the delivery of some 3,000 slaves to the colonies in the West Indies. Yet his significance was greater than the bare statistics suggest. Irving was one of an estimated 779 slave ship captains who 'traded at one time out of Liverpool' between 1785 and the abolition of the trade in 1807.[7] He was, therefore, one of the many individuals, European and American, whose career ambitions and personal expectations were intimately bound up with the transatlantic trade in slaves.

Irving's success in this expanding and profitable trade is reflected in the comparatively young age at which he was entrusted with his first ship by the large slaving firm of Baker and Dawson. Born on 15th December 1759, he was recorded as the master of the *Anna* when she was registered at Liverpool in April 1789.[8] In a recent study, Stephen Behrendt suggests that Liverpool slave ship captains born outside Lancashire were typically aged 31 before they attained command. Aged 29, Irving was more consistent with the pattern amongst Lancashire born captains who, on average, achieved their first command at 'just under twenty nine years of age...'[9]

Irving's training as a surgeon, however, differentiates him from the majority of Liverpool slave ship captains. Although other examples of surgeons appointed to command can be identified in the ports of Liverpool, Bristol and London, it was apparently still not common practice in the 1780s.[10] Case studies by Behrendt suggest that experience for captaincy was more typically gained as mariners and mates in the Liverpool West India trade followed by a period as mates on slave ships.[11] The career of Hugh Crow, a contemporary of Irving's, reflects a more typical progression fo slave ship captain. In his autobiography Crow describes how he served two years of an apprenticeship to a boat builder and was then apprenticed to a merchant, during which time he served on various ships trading to the West Indies, America and Norway. After completing his apprenticeship, Crow undertook several voyages as mate in the Liverpool West India trade before taking up his first appointment as chief mate on a slave ship in October 1790. His first captaincy was achieved in 1798 at the age of 33 after serving on six slaving voyages as a mate.[12] A comparison of James Irving's career with that of Hugh Crow reveals a number of similarities, as well as important differences.

Details of Irving's early education and professional training are sketchy. His later letters reveal that he was a man who derived immense pleasure from writing. His style is elegant, his vocabulary wide and his use of prose accomplished. The descriptive power of his writing is one of the most striking features of this correspondence and is a factor which contributes to the impression of a man of liberal education. At first sight his background, as the son of a smith turned innkeeper from Langholm, a small and fairly remote market town in a pastoral farming district, does not seem entirely consistent with this impression.[13]

The education received by his first cousin, David Irving, author of *The History of Scottish Poetry*, provides some indication of the opportunities that may have been open to James Irving in Langholm. Editorial comment accompanying an edition of this work published in Edinburgh in 1861 indicates that David Irving was educated at the grammar school in Langholm in the late eighteenth century by a '... skilful and successful master'. More interestingly, reference is made to the master of a private school in New Langholm named Andrew Little 'who had lost his sight by lightning on the coast of Africa, when surgeon of a Liverpool vessel...' Although Andrew Little was buried in Langholm in May 1803, it is not clear how long he had been in the town and whether he had any professional or personal contact with the subject of this text.[14] One might speculate that it was Andrew Little who directed James Irving to the trade with which he was obviously familiar.

The interval between James Irving's early education in Langholm and his first voyage out of the port of Liverpool in the early 1780s must remain a matter of some speculation. Although in later correspondence he refers to the fact that 'I was bred a surgeon originally...' there is no evidence to indicate where he received his training (Letter 11). Official reference to his status as surgeon is available only in 1789. In the examinations book of the Company of Surgeons, the predecessor of the Royal College of Surgeons of England, James Irving is bracketed together with four other individuals who were all passed as 'Surgeons to African ships' on 2nd April 1789. This does not imply that he was a Member of the Company of Surgeons, as the certificate granted was a much lower qualification.[15]

Details of Irving's early career in the Liverpool slave trade can be built up from a number of different sources, although the date at which he left the Scottish Borders and arrived in the rapidly expanding port is not recorded. William Lempriere, a doctor with whom James Irving later became acquainted, described how:[16]

...his first essay in the world was as a surgeon to a Guinea-man; after having made several voyages in this capacity, however, finding it a disadvantageous employment, he obtained the command of a small vessel in the same trade, and this was his first voyage as commander.

Crew lists or muster rolls indicate that prior to attaining his first captaincy, James Irving undertook at least seven voyages from the port of Liverpool between January 1782 and January 1789:[17]

Table 1. Voyages undertaken by James Irving, January 1782 — January 1789.

Ship	Captain	Destination	Date Entered	Date Discharged
Prosperity	James Murphy	Tortola	Jan. 1782	Sept. 1782
Vulture	William Wilson	Tortola	Nov. 1782	July 1783
Vulture	William Wilson	Jamaica	July 1783	May 1784
Jane	Quayle Fargher	Jamaica	Aug. 1784	July 1785
Jane	Quayle Fargher	Tobago	May 1786	Feb. 1787
Princess Royal	William Sherwood	Africa & Havana	Apr. 1787	Dec. 1787
Princess Royal	William Sherwood	Havana	Apr. 1788	Jan. 1789

Muster rolls indicate that Irving was entered on board the *Vulture* on 26th July 1783 for a voyage that showed the characteristic outline of the triangular trade in slaves (see Map 2).[18] After embarking from the port of Liverpool in the summer of 1783, *Lloyd's List* of 23rd January 1784 recorded that the ship was at Bonny in the Bight of Benin (see Map 3). Allowing for a time delay in news reaching London, this suggests that the *Vulture* reached the west coast of Africa in the latter months of 1783. In the edition of 23rd April 1784, this shipping newspaper records that the *Vulture* in the command of Captain Wilson had arrived at Barbados from Africa. This route from Africa to the West Indies, known as the 'Middle Passage', is entirely consistent with the assertion that this was a slaving voyage. Irving listed fourth out of a total muster of 66 men was presumably engaged as the ship's surgeon, although the muster roll does not, as usual, specify crew responsibilities. As crew members were listed hierarchically after the captain though, this suggests that on his first slaving venture, Irving held a position of some responsibility on the ship.

Although Lempriere's account of Irving's career development is substantially correct, he was not necessarily accurate in stating that his first voyage was in the slave trade. In common with Crow, Irving's career at sea may have included voyages in the Liverpool West India trade. Muster rolls reveal that an individual named James Irving was listed on an earlier voyage of the *Vulture* with Captain William Wilson between 7th November 1782 and 3rd July 1783.[19] The shipping intelligence in *Lloyd's List*, if complete, indicates that on this occasion the ship

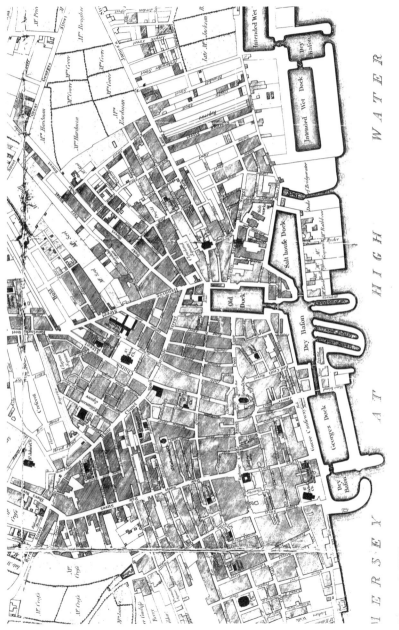

Liverpool, 1785. (courtesy of Liverpool Libraries & Information Services)

sailed directly from Liverpool to Tortola, one of the Virgin Islands, with no recorded visit to Africa 'en route'.[20] This is not surprising as many ships, and the seamen who manned them, alternated between the slave trade and the direct trade with Africa and the West Indies.[21] A still earlier muster list records that an individual named James Irving was entered on board the *Prosperity* for a voyage to Tortola with Captain James Murphy on 31st January 1782 and discharged just over seven months later on 23rd September 1782.[22] As James Irving was a fairly common name, it is difficult to be certain that these two earlier voyages in the direct trade to the West Indies relate to the subject of this study. Still, the evidence does indicate that Irving undertook his first slaving venture on the ship *Vulture* at the age of 22 or 23.

Quayle Fargher, who captained three slaving ventures between 1784 and 1787, served as chief mate on the *Vulture* between November 1782 and May 1784. When Fargher was given command of his first ship, the *Jane*, in the summer of 1784 'Mr. James Irving' was listed on board in his service. Irving was one of five men, other than the captain, whose names were prefixed by a status description which again suggests a position of seniority.[23] Personal contacts seemed, then, to have played some part in the way in which a crew was selected. Irving made contacts early in his career which proved useful when he was given command of his own ship a number of years later. On the second voyage with Quayle Fargher between May 1786 and February 1787, an individual named John Clegg was promoted from his former position as a seaman to one of mate. When Irving was given command of the *Anna* in 1789, it was Clegg that he chose for his first mate. Joseph Pearson, a seaman on the *Jane* was also recruited for the voyage of the *Anna*.[24]

It was on the second of these voyages on the *Jane* with Captain Fargher that Irving began the regular correspondence with his wife, Mary, which provides such a detailed insight into his slaving ventures. The timing of these letters may indicate that James Irving married Mary Tunstall in the unusually long interval between his discharge from the *Jane* on 2nd July 1785 and his re-entry onto the ship ten months later on 17th May 1786.[25] The first of these letters, addressed to his wife Mary at 9 College Lane, Liverpool, was written as the ship sailed from port on 19th May 1786. The letter powerfully conveys the sadness he felt at the separation from his wife, and of all the surviving letters this is by far the most personal and intimate to the extent that he urged Mary to 'show no person this letter, it is not fit to be seen' (Letter 1).

By the time the *Jane* reached Tobago seven months later in December 1786, Irving confided to his wife, Mary, his intention of finding another kind of employment (Letter 4). He outlined that:

I'm nearly wearied of this unnatural accursed trade and think (if no change of station takes place) when convenience suits of adopting some other mode of life, although I'm fully sensible and aware of the difficultys attending any new undertaking, yet I will at least look around me.

In spite of these reservations though, Irving was entered on board the *Princess Royal* in April 1787, less than two months after he returned to Liverpool with the ship *Jane*.[26] This may suggest that he was unable to find an alternative form of employment with comparable remuneration or that he was offered the prospect of promotion or enhanced reward on a larger ship.

The *Princess Royal*, built in John Barton's shipyard in Liverpool in 1783, was the largest ship owned by the merchants Peter Baker and John Dawson.[27] The Certificate of British Registry described the vessel as a 'frigate built ship' of 596 tons burthen with:[28]

... two decks and three masts, that her length from the fore part of the main stem to the after part of the stern – post aloft is one hundred and twenty seven feet, her breadth at the broadest part ... thirty three feet six inches ... her height between decks six feet ... has large quarter gallerys and a female figure head.

The use of the term 'frigate built' indicates that the ship had a raised deck at the stern of the vessel. As the *Princess Royal* was capable of carrying more than 800 slaves, this was an important safety feature for the crew giving an elevated observation and defence position in case of riot.[29]

His first voyage to Africa and Havana with Captain William Sherwood lasted just over eight months, after which Irving was entered on the same ship for a second voyage to Havana on 10th April 1788.[30] In a document dated 26th March 1788, in which he appointed his wife, Mary, as his 'true and lawful attorney' to administer his affairs in his absence, Irving described himself as 'Surgeon of the ship *Princess Royal*'.[31] James Irving was probably influential in the decision to engage another surgeon for this voyage. Although a pragmatic decision in view of the huge slave carrying capacity of the *Princess Royal*, personal contacts again played a part as the surgeon engaged was Irving's younger cousin and namesake, also from Langholm in Scotland. Aged 15 or 16, James Irving II was listed ninth out of a total muster of 83 men, two places below his more experienced cousin.

Shortly after setting sail from Liverpool, James Irving informed his wife Mary that the ship was bound for Bonny on the west coast of Africa. With his usual concern for his wife's peace of mind, he reassured her that 'the ship proves very well so that you have nothing to fear from her late misfortune'.[32] No further details of this misfortune are provided in this badly damaged letter, although it is clear from the contents that he had informed her of the circumstances in previous correspondence (Letter 7). A letter written by his younger cousin though, discovered in the private ownership of a distant kinsman in Langholm, paints a fuller picture of the circumstances associated with the sailing of the *Princess Royal* in the spring of 1788. (Letter 8) As the ship made ready to sail from Liverpool, he wrote to his parents, Janetus and Helen Irving of Langholm, and described how:

> We would have sailed long before this but as the ship [deleted] was going out of the dock into the river on the 23rd of last month, it being past high water and no wind, the strength of the tide turned her round and ran her aground and left her there till next tide. And she being so sharp bottomed lay on one side, which so strained her that she was all bent and leaked very much and she has been in the river ever since. But now she is straight and leaks so little that there is scarce enough to wash the decks and in the course of a month we expect there will be none. But, however, if it should continue it can do us no harm.

This may well have been his first voyage. The tone of the letter to his parents, the minor domestic details he describes of his sleeping arrangements and the items that he has been given for his cabin, all convey something of the novelty of his experience.[33]

The voyage of the *Princess Royal* in 1788 would have partly fulfilled the terms of a legal contract or 'asiento' with the Spanish government in which John Dawson undertook to supply slaves to Spain's American colonies.[34] In a petition to the House of Lords dated 10th July 1788 John Dawson described how earlier that year he had entered into a 'contract with his Spanish Majesty for supplying slaves to the Spanish West India Islands' and was 'bound under very heavy penalties to import into the Spanish West Indies not less than 3000 slaves annually'. The *Princess Royal* was the most important vessel amongst the 'five ships employed in the African Trade, the smallest of which is 325 tons and the largest 596 tons burthen...'. These ships were 'all frigate built and particularly constituted for the purpose of accommodating the slaves, none of such ships being less than 5' 10" between decks'. This was not a new commitment though, as in the same petition Dawson indicates that together with Peter Baker he had entered into a similar arrangement in 1784 'to supply the Spanish West India Islands with not less than 5,000 slaves annually'. Under the terms of this contract they 'delivered upwards of 11,000 slaves ... for which they received dollars which they imported into this kingdom'. In a petition presented to the House a week earlier, Dawson estimated that this contract had been worth upwards of £350,000.[35]

Shipping information in *Lloyd's List* of 28th October 1788 indicates that the *Princess Royal* arrived at Trinidad from Africa on 26th August 1788 'with about

800 slaves for Havannah'. At a time when Sherwood and his crew would have been heavily involved in the purchase of slaves on the African coast in the summer of 1788, John Dawson, their employer, was engaged in petitioning Parliament to retain the right to transport such large numbers of slaves to the Spanish colonies. In two petitions presented to the House of Lords in July 1788, it is clear that John Dawson was concerned that the terms of legislation before Parliament would interfere with his ability to fulfil his Spanish contracts. He argued that:

> ... if the said bill passes into a law in its present form the ships employed by your petitioner will be rendered useless and as your petitioner according to the terms of the before mentioned contract cannot employ smaller ships, therefore your petitioner will be prevented from compleating the said contract and will thereby not only incur considerable penalties, but the property now embarked by your petitioner and the said Peter Baker in the African Trade will be lost, and your petitioner has great reason to apprehend that he and the said Peter Baker will be totally ruined.

The cause of his concern stemmed from proposed regulations to limit the number of slaves that could be carried. He argued, seemingly altruistically, that far from protecting the slaves, their welfare would be adversely affected by the legislation:[36]

> That the bill now depending before your Lordships restrains the proportion of five slaves to three tons only to the first 201 tons after which the vessels above that tonnage are to take but one slave for every ton exceeding whereby the small ships which are less adapted to this trade will have advantage over the larger vessels though the former will be much more lumbered with their materials and furniture as they must contain every article which the largest ships can need at sea and thereby be less benefitted by fresh air and fewer conveniencies of room, and are liable to greater motion from the sea than larger vessels to the great discomfit of the slaves unused to water conveyance, and are much longer detained on the coast than large vessels are, because these by reason of their force dare enter the largest harbours whereas the small vessels generally frequent only the lesser harbours and by reason of their small force and small compliment of hands the crews of such small vessels are very frequently cut off by the natives and the slaves are also more easily tempted to insurrection, and therefore, your petitioner conceives that the present bill instead of relieving the slaves will, by the discouragement given to large vessels be pregnant with mischief to and occasion the destruction and murder of the whites and the slaves not relieved as small ships cannot carry cargoe and stoars for the compliment they are allowed by the Act.

Probably of more pressing concern to John Dawson however, was the fact that if the proposed regulations came into force a ship such as the *Princess Royal* would be forced to reduce the number of slaves carried by at least seventy.[37]

The voyage of the *Princess Royal* to Havana in 1788 satisfied one quarter of the minimum requirement of 3,000 slaves specified in Dawson's agreement with the Spanish government. Assuming the ship also landed 800 slaves at Havana in 1787, the two voyages in which Irving participated accounted for more than one-tenth of the 11,000 slaves landed in Spanish colonies by Baker and Dawson between 1784 and 1788.

On the first of these two voyages with Captain William Sherwood, Irving wrote to his wife Mary from Havana in Cuba on 20th October 1787 (Letter 6). He makes no mention of the number of slaves carried, but does indicate that they were awaiting payment at Havana:

> Adieu, I think I shall chase this [the letter] very hard, if the dollars don't detain us. How that will be I cannot say, but hope their treasury will receive a fresh supply before we are ready. If so await me...

He describes Havana to his wife as a 'strongly fortified, almost impregnable' city and that '30 sail of the line and 30,000 men would not be able to force a surrender'. The letter though, is mostly concerned with news of a personal nature, including his comment that 'the Spanish beef and cabbage have wonderfull effects on an exhausted sailor after the long [...] African voyage'. He informs his wife that they hope to leave Havana on 1st November 1787 and that she should expect the ship by Christmas. His estimation was broadly correct as *Williamson's Liverpool Advertiser* of Monday 7th January 1788 records that the ship arrived in Liverpool 'from Africa and Havanna with 4 elephant teeth, 11 bags cotton, 1496 cow hides for Baker and Dawson'.

James Irving's conduct on these two voyages must have impressed the captain, William Sherwood, who later described him '... to be as carefull, sober and industrious a man as ever lived'. Sherwood's comments in a letter of 2nd May 1790 correspond with the information in the muster rolls as he points out 'I've had an opportunity of knowing him well, he haveing been two voyages with me to Africa'. As Sherwood was himself described as amongst '...the most respectable commanders in the African Trade ... in the employ of Messrs. Baker and Dawson', his favourable opinion may well have been influential in the decision to offer Irving command of the *Anna* in 1789.[38] Hugh Crow certainly attributed his appointment as chief mate on the *Prince*, also a Baker and Dawson ship, to the 'recommendations of the two captains with whom I had last sailed'.[39]

Irving's experience in the slave trade built up over the previous six years, combined with his medical training, was of particular relevance to his employer.

In the summer of 1788 newly introduced legislation stated that there should be at least one surgeon on board a slave ship with a 'certificate of his having passed his examination at Surgeons Hall'. Clause XI of the 'Act to regulate ... the shipping and carrying of slaves in British vessels from the coast of Africa' also stipulated that a master of a slave ship should have previous experience in the trade. The legislation, more widely referred to as Dolben's Act, specified that the master of a slave ship should have served on one previous voyage in that capacity, as chief mate or surgeon during two whole previous voyages, or as chief or other mate in three voyages:[40]

> That from and after the first day of August one thousand seven hundred and eighty-eight, it shall not be lawful for any person to become a master, or to take or have the command or charge of any such ship or vessel at the time she shall clear out from any port of Great Britain for purchasing and carrying slaves from the coast of Africa, unless such master ... shall have already served in such capacity during one voyage, or shall have served as chief mate or surgeon during the whole of two voyages, or either as chief or other mate, during three voyages, in purchasing and carrying slaves from the coast of Africa; under pain that such master, or person taking or having charge or command of any such ship or vessel, and also the owner or owners, who shall hire or employ such person, shall, for every such offence respectively, forfeit and pay the sum of fifty pounds.

Irving's qualifications and experience satisfied both stipulations. The offer of command to Irving was possibly linked to the timing of legislative control of the slave trade, although it did make good economic sense to appoint a man with medical knowledge to the command of a slave ship.[41] Irving's voyage on the *Anna*, a ship which may have been purpose built for the slave trade, irrevocably changed his life and career aspirations. As this voyage represented a markedly different phase in Irving's career, it will be the subject of separate discussion below.

In summary then, James Irving's traceable career at sea was based largely on the slave trade. Like many other Liverpool captains though, he may well have undertaken several voyages in the direct West India trade. The main focus of his activities before the offer of a command was as a surgeon, as he completed five slaving voyages in this capacity between July 1783 and January 1789, two of which were on the largest vessel in the fleet of Baker and Dawson. During this time he seems to have gained the trust and confidence of Captain William Sherwood, one of the leading Liverpool slave captains, whom he came to regard as a personal friend.[42] On the basis of the impression that he made with his superior officers during these five voyages, he was credited with having the personal character traits necessary to command a ship. The position of captain offered the prospect of enhanced financial reward, particularly through the payment of a commission from the sale of the slaves.[43] Irving may have planned to complete a number of voyages as captain and use the profits to establish himself as a merchant, although recent research shows that the odds were against him as the many dangers of the African trade were such that 'five captains died in the trade for every one who attained the status of merchant'.[44]

Individual career patterns of the type outlined for James Irving can largely be built up from muster rolls, shipping information in newspapers and biographical details contained in parish registers.[45] What is exceptional in Irving's case is the detailed record of his voyages contained in the letters he sent regularly to his wife, Mary. It is indeed rare to find personal records or correspondence of the captains who were actively involved in the eighteenth century slave trade. This newly discovered evidence provides an in-depth view of Irving's activities and attitudes and, as such, can be set beside the well-known accounts of the slave trade by John Newton and Hugh Crow. Irving's letters, written from various locations in Africa and the West Indies, provide a very personal and individual view of the slave trade. In many respects Irving's experience is not subject to generalisation; in fact the great strength of this archive lies in its personal nature. Often though, he unwittingly provides information that elucidates key features of the late eighteenth century slave trade.

3. Characteristics of the slave trade.

The sequence of letters from each voyage undertaken by Irving highlight the familiar outline of the 'triangular trade'.[1] Common to each voyage was the purchase of slaves on the west coast of Africa, their re-sale in the West Indies and the return journey to Liverpool with bills of exchange to be drawn against a British merchant house and/or a cargo from the Caribbean and Africa.[2] Although these are well studied characteristics of the slave trade, Irving's letters shed some light on the complexities of the trade and the variable elements within this deceptively simple pattern.

Other than the obvious variables of wind and weather, the time taken to complete a voyage was influenced by a range of factors often outside the control of the captain and crew. On average ships took just over eleven months to complete the three-cornered route in the 1790s.[3] Turnaround times on the African coast were dependent on the availability of slaves, the organisation of supply and the terms of trade. On 13th August 1786 at New Calabar in the Bight of Biafra, Irving expressed his frustration that they would be delayed on the coast for a further two months (see Map 3). The *Jane* in the command of Captain

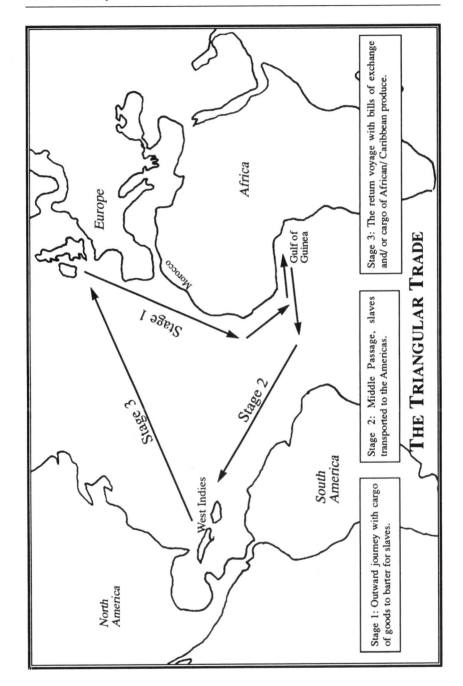

Stage 1: Outward journey with cargo of goods to barter for slaves.

Stage 2: Middle Passage, slaves transported to the Americas.

Stage 3: The return voyage with bills of exchange and/ or cargo of African/ Caribbean produce.

THE TRIANGULAR TRADE

Fargher had arrived there a month earlier after a voyage of approximately two months from Liverpool and Irving's comment that 'trade is dull ...' implies that they were experiencing some difficulty in obtaining a sufficient number or quality of slaves (Letter 2). The ship finally left the African coast early in October 1786, which suggests that almost three months had been spent obtaining a cargo.[4]

According to *Lloyd's List* of 26th January 1787 a final cargo of 526 slaves reached Tobago. As Irving informed his wife, Mary, on his arrival in the West Indies on 22nd November 1786 that they had 'buried 48 slaves', this suggests that 574 slaves were purchased on the African coast, although some further allowance may have to be made for those who died whilst the *Jane* lay off the coast of Africa (Letter 3).[5]

Captain Fargher, accompanied by the ship's surgeon, Irving, would have exchanged an assortment of manufactured goods from the ship's cargo for slaves. The slaves assembled on the coast by African traders or merchants using complex structures of delivery, were typically exchanged for textiles, copper, brass and pewter goods, beads, guns, gunpowder and liquor.[6] Textiles and metals were normally the most important commodities of exchange, although regional differences in taste along the west coast of Africa affected the precise ratio of different types of goods.[7] David Richardson emphasises that the skill of the captain in negotiating a favourable rate of exchange for these trade goods was central to the financial success of the voyage.[8] The final number of slaves carried on the *Jane*, at least 574, may have been built up by regular purchases of small numbers, more infrequent purchases from large scale suppliers or through a number of sources of supply with different characteristics. As P. E H. Hair points out 'slaves were offered to shippers directly or through European agents resident on the coast, sometimes by notables, sometimes by lesser men, but most commonly by traders'.[9]

The manner in which slaves were obtained, differed along the African coast. New Calabar, where the *Jane* was anchored when Irving wrote to his wife in August 1786, is located in the Bight of Biafra which centres on the area of the Niger delta (see Map 3). This region of the west coast was characterised by 'good harbours, large scale suppliers and perhaps more fundamentally, their slave trade derived from regular hinterland sources'. B.K. Drake, a historian of the slave trade, comments that '... in the most effective loading region, a ship could, more often than not, obtain 300 slaves in from 75 to 150 days ...'.[10] With a minimum total of 574 slaves obtained over a period of approximately 90 days, the *Jane* demonstrated a high loading rate of approximately six to seven slaves a day. This is an average figure and gives little indication of the mechanisms of trade and the regularity of supply. In spite of the delays referred to by Irving, the stay of three months on the coast by the *Jane* is consistent with the average length of stay of ships in the Niger delta of 91 days between 1791-7.[11]

On a later voyage on board the *Princess Royal*, Irving wrote to his wife on 3rd June 1787 from 'Bonney river', also in the Bight of Biafra, informing her that they had arrived five days previously. His comment that 'we broke trade yesterday' indicates that they had already made the customary present or 'dash' to the local notable and that the process of bartering their cargo for slaves had commenced.[12] Irving estimated that this would take nine or ten weeks to complete (Letter 5). If this was an accurate assessment it suggests that turn-around times in the Niger delta could be significantly faster than the average time cited above. On the other hand, the experience of the *Dobson* eighteen years earlier indicates that trading could be protracted. During a period of almost six months from July 1769 to January 1770 566 slaves were purchased, typically in small numbers of between one and three individuals. Antera Duke of Old Calabar, familiar to historians as he wrote a diary covering the years 1785-1788, was one of the thirty African traders who sold slaves to the ship. Antera Duke was fairly typical of the other traders as he sold 37 slaves in 15 separate transactions between 31st July and 12th December 1769. In return, he received payment in various types of imported goods including cloth, iron bars and gunpowder. This 'African entrepreneur' may well have sold other items to the ship, such as ivory for export and yams and other foodstuffs for provisions.[13]

The African destinations mentioned by Irving in his letters were amongst the most popular trading locations with British ships in the last two decades of the century. Of the estimated 766,000 slaves exported by British ships in this period, David Richardson considers that about half (380,000) were obtained in the Bight of Biafra, which included Bonny, Old Calabar and New Calabar. Of growing importance was the area classified as West Central Africa which accounted for over 150,000 slaves exported in British ships between 1780-1799. This south-eastward shift in trade was pronounced in the later decades of the century, although none of the voyages in which Irving was employed apparently visited this area. Over 80,000 of the slaves exported on British ships were obtained on the Gold Coast and, although not an important trading region, this was the principal area from which Captain Irving obtained slaves during a voyage he undertook in 1791.[14]

More detailed evidence of Irving's activities on the African coast can be found from this voyage of the *Ellen*, which sailed from Liverpool on 2nd January 1791. Specific information is available for this, his second captaincy of a slave ship, as the *Ellen* is one of approximately 350 ships listed in the 'Return to an Order of the Right Honourable the House of Lords dated 10th July 1799' in which the Clerk of the Parliament had been directed to extract several categories of information from the 'several log books and journals of ships employed in the slave trade in each year from 1791 to 1797...'.[15] This records that the *Ellen* arrived at Anamabu on the Gold Coast of Africa on 5th April 1791, and after an atypically long stay of more than five months on the coast, departed from the same location on 16th September 1791. During this period a total of 341 slaves were purchased, indicating an average loading rate of approximately two slaves per day. As with any average this figure conceals the extremes, as the number of slaves loaded varied from the large single consignment of 58 females and 29 males on 11th April 1791 down to just one female on 18th August 1791.[16]

As it was not uncommon practice for ships to trade between a small number of locations on the coast, these slaves may have been purchased at a number of different trading centres. A letter written by the ship's surgeon, Captain Irving's cousin and namesake, gives some clues to the movement of the *Ellen* along the African coast (Letter 37). In a letter written as the *Ellen* made ready to sail from Liverpool, James Irving II informed his parents, Janetus and Helen Irving in Langholm, that:[17]

> We are bound for Anamaboe in the Gold Coast, discharge what goods we have for that place and set sail from it again within 48 hours after we arrived. Then we are to call at Lagus, Accra and other parts whose names I have forgot. We are then to go down as far as Benin river and stay a day or two and then go back to Anamaboe from which place we are to sail for the West Indies.

In broad outline, James Irving II's account is consistent with the details in the House of Lords lists as the ship did in fact arrive at Anamabu and depart from the same location. This points to the overall reliability of the surgeon's account, which was probably based on the instructions that his cousin, the captain, had received from John Dawson.

Details extracted from the log and journal of the *Ellen* by the Clerk of the Parliament indicate that the first group of 87 slaves was received on 11th April 1791, six days after their stated arrival at Anamabu. Comparing this with the account by James Irving II, indicates that these slaves were probably obtained at one of the more easterly locations of Accra on the Gold Coast or Lagos in the Bight of Benin (see Map 3). The surgeon's letter gives no indication whether some other type of trading, possibly for food or exports such as ivory, was intended during their initial two day stay at Anamabu. Most of the slaves obtained on 11th April were, however, transferred to another ship on 26th April with a further seven transhipped on 24th May 1791. These inter-ship transactions left just five female slaves on board the *Ellen* until further purchases of slaves were made in July. This pattern may indicate that prior to sailing with his own cargo of slaves for the West Indies, Captain Irving carried out instructions to supply slaves to another Baker and Dawson ship on the coast.

The timing and pattern of Hugh Crow's first slaving venture on the *Prince* is very similar to the movement of the *Ellen* along the west coast of Africa, although there is no evidence to indicate that Crow and Irving met during this period. After overcoming his initial antipathy to the slave trade, Crow accepted a position as 'chief mate of a beautiful brig belonging to J. Dawson Esq. called the *Prince...*' The ship sailed from Liverpool in October 1790 and reached Anamabu after a passage of seven weeks. Crow records that 'we lay there about three weeks before transacting any trade, the king of that part of the coast having died some time before, in consequence of which, all business was suspended'. Following this delay they 'proceeded to a place called Lago with negroes, and thence to Benin. We traded between both places for several months, so that I acquired a considerable knowledge, as a pilot, of that part of the coast'. Crow's description indicates that some slaves were eventually purchased at Anamabu and that they were taken along the coast to Lagos, possibly for transfer to another ship. The account implies that the *Prince* experienced some difficulty in securing a sufficient cargo of slaves as 'the agents who were employed on different parts of the coast by our owner, Mr. Dawson, having all fallen victims to the climate in a few months after their arrival...' Curtin argues that 'Europeans newly arrived at trading posts on the Gulf of Guinea usually sustained a death rate of about 50% in the first year of residence'.[18] Crow records that 'in order that we might convey to him the melancholy news as soon as possible, we took in a quantity of ivory and other articles and sailed from Benin'.[19]

Captain Irving wrote to his wife on 14th June 1791 on board the' *Ellen* off Benin Barr' which confirms the pattern of the voyage that his younger cousin and ship's surgeon had communicated to his parents in Langholm (Letter 40). The surgeon had stated that they would only 'go down as far as Benin river and stay a day or two and then go back to Anamaboe ...' As no further slave purchases were recorded until 2nd July 1791, this suggests that Anamabu was the principal location at which they obtained their cargo. The evidence extracted from the surgeon's journal and ship's log suggests that in the period from 2nd July to September 14th 1791 effort was concentrated on securing a cargo for the *Ellen* as only three of the 253 slaves purchased in this period were transferred to other ships.

Progress in obtaining a cargo was particularly slow in the month of August as only one slave was added to the total of 111 purchased in July. This delay may have been occasioned by the loss of the agents on the coast described by Crow, which may have forced Irving to purchase directly from African suppliers. As the *Prince* only reached Liverpool in August 1791 to convey the 'melancholy news', there would have been no time for the merchants to replace those agents who had

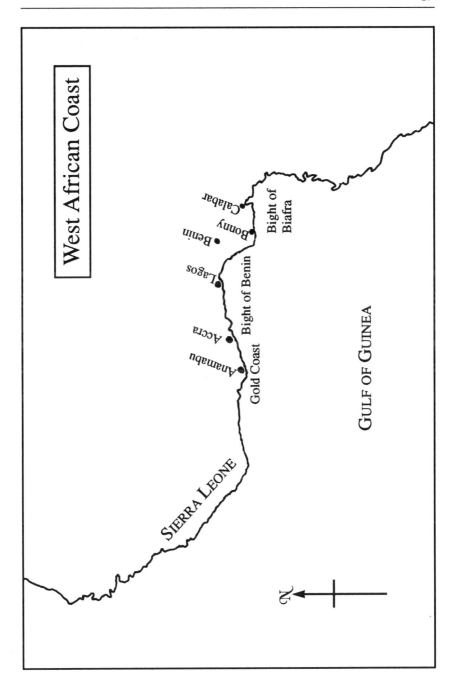

West African Coast

SIERRA LEONE

Anamabu
Accra
Lagos
Benin
Bonny
Calabar

Gold Coast
Bight of Benin
Bight of Biafra

GULF OF GUINEA

N

died on the coast. September was by far the most successful month as Irving managed to load 142 slaves in a 14 day period. This was partly facilitated by two large receipts of 70 slaves on 9th September and 50 slaves three days later. In July the numbers acquired were typically much smaller, ranging from 30 slaves on 2nd July down to 12 the following day. The variations in loading patterns in this ten week period tend to suggest that Captain Irving acquired slaves using a variety of different methods. Unfortunately, neither Captain Irving nor his cousin make any reference in their letters to the manner in which they acquired the slaves. The letters are silent about the transactions involved and the nature of the contact that both men, each trained as a surgeon, must have had with the slaves. Before any purchases were made, for example, they would have examined the slaves who were stripped naked for inspection, to assess their medical state and suitability for re-sale.[20]

The profits of the triangular trade were largely dependent, though not wholly, on the number of slaves that were fit for re-sale in the West Indies.[21] The effectiveness of the surgeon in controlling the level of illness or deaths amongst the slaves cannot be quantified, and the measures that a surgeon might take to control illness and disease on board ship find no mention in the letters of James Irving and his cousin.[22] Following a journey from Africa to the West Indies on board the *Jane* with Captain Fargher in 1787, Irving informs his wife that they had buried 48 slaves. This percentage loss of 8% is small compared to Irving's later voyage on the *Ellen*. No deaths of slaves on the African coast were recorded, but of the 253 slaves that left Africa on board the *Ellen* in September 1791 only 206 survived the Middle Passage. This figure is high compared to an average mortality of 5.7% amongst British ships engaged in the slave trade between 1791 and 1797. On average those British ships which obtained slaves from the Gold Coast, where Anamabu is located, showed an average slave mortality of 2.7%, which again tends to emphasise the high losses on board the *Ellen*.[23]

The loss of almost one-fifth of the slaves (19%) meant that neither the captain nor the surgeon on this voyage qualified for the payment of the bounty introduced by the Dolben Act of 1788, as the slave deaths far exceeded the maximum level of 3% needed to qualify for a bonus.[24] The surgeon had clearly taken this lump sum into account in his personal financial calculations. As the *Ellen* prepared to leave Liverpool, the surgeon informed his parents that '... if it please God we make a good voyage I ~~expect to~~ get head money and if we only bury 6 slaves my cousin will receive £100 and I £50 [?]bounty. If we bury not more than 9 slaves my couzen will receive £50 and I £25 bounty'(Letter 37).

An outbreak of disease may explain the high proportion of slave deaths recorded on the *Ellen*. The flux or dysentery was the cause of death most commonly referred to by slave traders and it is possible that amoebic dysentery, the 'bloody flux' referred to by various commentators, could have been introduced onto the ship in contaminated water or food supplies or by slaves who were incubating the disease. This form of dysentery had an incubation period of between 20 and 90 days and the infected individual could experience frequent recurrence of the symptoms. The inexorable spread of disease on board ship is forcefully conveyed in John Newton's dispassionate record of slave deaths on the *Duke of Argyle* by their allotted purchase number. He records on 21st April 1751 that he 'was obliged to waive the consideration of the day [the religious service for the crew] for the first and, I hope, the last time of the voyage, the season advancing fast and, I am afraid sickness too, for we have almost every day one or more taken with a flux, of which a woman dyed tonight (No. 79)'.[25] Other common causes of deaths amongst slaves included yellow fever and communicable illnesses such as measles and smallpox, although it has recently been argued that dehydration was 'by far the biggest cause of slave mortality during the Middle Passage'. This interpretation suggests that the excessive heat and poor ventilation below decks combined with seasickness, dysentery and inadequate supplies of water caused dehydration amongst slaves.[26]

If disease had been present on board the *Ellen* during the voyage to Trinidad, the contagion could have spread rapidly in the space between decks where the slaves spent a large proportion of their time. The Certificate of British Registry indicates that the tween deck height of the *Ellen* was considerably lower than standing room at just 4 feet, 1' 8" lower than the more well-known case of the slave ship *Brookes*. One commentator observed that slaves were so tightly packed into the holds of ships that:[27]

> they had not so much room as a man in a coffin. They were placed lying on their back, and sometimes they were packed spoonways, one on the other; so close were they, you could not walk without treading on them.

If the information extracted from the surgeon's log was an accurate record of numbers of slaves taken on board the *Ellen*, then the ship was not overcrowded by the standards established by Dolben's Act in 1788. The ship, a 'prize captured from Americans' in 1782 was described in the following terms in the Certificate of British Registry on 14th December 1790:[28]

> ...American built, has two decks and three masts, that her length from the fore part of the main stem to the after part of the taffrail aloft is seventy five feet ten inches. Her breadth at the broadest part...or below the main wales twenty two feet ten inches...her height between decks four feet and admeasures one hundred and fifty two tons and 42ths. That she is a square sterned ship with a

deep waist and a high quarter deck and pierced for sixteen guns. Has quarter badges and a figure.

The *Ellen*, a ship of 152 tons, was smaller than the average size of British vessels of 191 tons that operated on the Gold Coast between 1790 and 1797.[29] As it was less than 201 tons burthen, the *Ellen* was legally entitled to carry five slaves for every three tons of weight, in other words 1.67 per ton. With a final cargo of 253 slaves on its departure from the African coast, the *Ellen* was not technically overcrowded, but like most slave vessels had been filled to its maximum legal capacity.[30]

The promoters of the Dolben Act obviously believed that by limiting the number of slaves per ton that they would limit slave ship mortality, but the case of the *Ellen* indicates that even when the regulations were observed mortality could still be high. A number of quantitative studies of the British, French and Dutch trades in the eighteenth century have found no clear or direct relationship between mortality levels and the number of slaves carried per ton. In other words tight packing or crowding of slaves, although it could contribute to the spread of disease, does not adequately explain the patterns of deaths amongst slaves carried by ships of different nations in the Middle Passage.[31] Some writers have suggested that the place of origin of the slaves and the epidemiological environment from which they were drawn might hold the key, whilst others have posited length of voyage as an important factor which affected slave mortality.[32]

The *Ellen* spent 117 days in the Middle Passage and it is possible that shortage of provisions and water on a longer than expected voyage affected survival rates amongst the slaves. Klein and Engerman in a study of the French slave trade found that voyages ranging from 121-140 days in the Middle Passage showed a high mortality rate of 18.6%, which is very close to the level of 19% recorded for the *Ellen*.[33]

Those who argued in favour of abolition of the trade, expressed concern not only about the slaves but also for the well-being of crew members. Falconbridge, for example, pointed out in 1788 that 'the evils attendant on this inhuman traffick, are not confined to the purchased negroes'. He argued that 'the sufferings of the seamen employed in the slave trade from the unwholesomeness of the climate, the inconveniences of the voyage, the brutal severity of the commanders, and other causes, fall very little short, nor prove in proportion to the numbers, less destructive to the sailors than negroes'.[34] The loss of seamen in the 'triangular trade' was an important argument used in the parliamentary session of 1788 to discredit the slave trade. It was claimed, for example, that of the 3,170 seamen who left Liverpool for Africa in 1786, less than a half returned (1,428).[35]

The voyage of the *Jane* in which Irving was engaged between 1786 and 1787 recorded a much higher proportion of returners of almost three-quarters, and although not statistically significant, it does suggest caution in the use of the abolitionists' statistics. Taking the voyage as a whole, all 43 members of the crew were entered on board in Liverpool on 17th May 1786, of whom 31 finally returned to Liverpool (72%). In total seven crew members died (16%), two of these during the three month stay on the coast of Africa and the remaining five during their stay in the West Indies and on the return voyage to Liverpool. No deaths are recorded in the course of the Middle Passage. A number of crew members were lost through desertion, mostly in the West Indies. The circumstances lying behind the events of 19th December 1786 are not explained in the bare listing of facts in the muster roll of the *Jane*. William Cock, Edward Griffiths and Joseph Guy all deserted the ship on that day. Nicholas Brown died on the same day and William Cenco was 'discharged' from the ship. John Collins, a seaman, deserted the ship five days later on Christmas Eve.[36] In a letter to his wife, written from Tobago on 2nd December 1786, Irving informs her that there had been some delay in the sale of the slaves and that 'I'm pretty certain of eating my Christmas dinner here (if able to eat one)'. The dates indicate that the desertions occurred in Tobago and may have resulted from frustration at the delay in sailing (Letter 4).

Although the muster rolls periodically record drownings amongst the crew, the major risk to mariners in the 'triangular trade' was that posed by disease. In letters written on board the *Jane, Princess Royal* and *Ellen*, Irving repeatedly comments on his own health and that of the officers. Though this was an obvious predisposition in a surgeon, the tone of his comments does suggest that the threat of illness was pervasive. In a letter from New Calabar dated 13th August 1786, for example, he informs his wife that 'We are all alive that left Liverpool and in health, one excepted who is dangerously ill' (Letter 3). Reference to the muster list of the ship *Jane* confirms that there were no recorded deaths on the first leg of the voyage to Africa. John Marvault who died on 30th August 1786 was the first of the two deaths recorded during their stay on the African coast, and it is likely that he was the 'dangerously ill' person referred to by Irving. He may have been suffering from malaria or yellow fever, to which Europeans were particularly susceptible on the African coast.[37]

During the voyage of the *Princess Royal* to Africa and Havana in 1787, eight of the 54 crew members died (15%). In a letter dated 3rd June 1787, Irving informs his wife that they arrived at Bonny River in Africa on 29th May 1787 (Letter 5). Reference to the muster roll for the ship shows that none of these deaths occurred on the outward voyage to the Niger delta. Most were concentrated in the period between 17th June and 2nd August 1787 which corresponds with the time on the African coast. Irving wrote to Mary from Havana on 20th October 1787 and informed her that 'Captain Sherwood and all our officers are well. We have buried 6 white people'(Letter 6). Reference to the muster roll confirms that the deaths were amongst the seamen rather than the officers named in the letters, but the total in the muster roll for the period between his letter of 2nd June and that of 20th October is seven rather than six. The eighth recorded death was that of William Coslett on 7th November 1787.[38]

Crew mortality was higher than that amongst the slaves during Irving's second voyage on the *Jane* between 17th May 1786 and 27th February 1787, as 16% of the crew members died compared to just over 8% of the slaves. Despite the heavy losses of slaves in the Middle Passage, this was also true of the later voyage of the *Ellen* as 22% of the crew members died (6 of 27) compared with 19% of the slaves (47 of 253).[39] These figures for the voyages in which Irving participated are broadly consistent with Curtin's estimate that 1 in 5 of the crew members were lost in the African trade and that the death rate was 'uniformly higher' than that amongst the slaves. Curtin describes the South Atlantic system as 'a cruel and wasteful operation – most damaging for the slaves themselves, but deadly even for those who were free and voluntary participants'.[40] Hugh Crow found it particularly offensive that a bounty was paid when there were few slave deaths but 'not a word was said about the white slaves and the poor sailors; these might die without regret'.[41] As Robert Stein points out in a study of the French slave trade, slaves 'were ultimately less dispensable than crew members in the search for a profitable trade. Captains were occasionally paid bonuses for keeping their slaves alive; they were never rewarded for keeping sailors alive'.[42]

The profitability of each voyage in which James Irving was involved cannot be calculated as there are no known surviving accounts.[43] The value of the slave trade to particular merchants, communities and the developing industrial economy of Britain as a whole has been extensively debated, although a consensus has yet to emerge. It is known that a number of the prominent merchant families in Liverpool accrued significant levels of wealth on the basis of the trade.[44]

The trade had its attendant risks though. David Richardson draws attention to the 'freakish' elements of the slave trade in which spectacular gains made in a handful of voyages could compensate for modest profits or even losses in other voyages.[45] An anonymous Liverpool writer in the late nineteenth century highlighted the unpredictable elements and the risks involved in the slave trade:[46]

... the African commerce holds forward one constant train of uncertainty, the time of slaving is precarious, the length of the Middle Passage uncertain, a vessel may be in part, or wholly cut off, mortalities may be great, and various other incidents may arise impossible to be forseen.

The shipwreck of the *Anna* on 27th May 1789, three and a half weeks after she sailed from Liverpool in the command of Captain James Irving, was a significant financial loss for John Dawson. Although only a small schooner of 50 tons burthen, it was a 'fine new vessell' completed earlier that year in a Liverpool shipyard and registered just 17 days before she sailed.[47] Dawson would have expended a considerable sum on building the ship, fitting it out for the slave trade and providing a crew and cargo.[48] Described as a 'square sterned schooner' in the Certificate of British Registry, the *Anna* was just one-tenth of the registered tonnage of the *Princess Royal*, the ship on which Irving had previously completed two voyages to Africa.

The small size of the *Anna* is particularly striking when compared to those ships which Dawson stated he owned in his petition to the House of Lords on 10th July 1788, the smallest of which was 325 tons. In this petition Dawson contended that the new legislation favoured smaller vessels, and the addition of the *Anna*, albeit shortlived, to his fleet may have been an attempt to respond to the restrictions imposed by Dolben's Act.[49] Under the terms of this Act, the *Anna* was capable of carrying just over 80 slaves, which was broadly equivalent to the reduction that the legislation had imposed on the *Princess Royal*. It is not known though whether Irving had received instructions from Dawson to sail the *Anna* from the west coast of Africa to one of the Spanish colonies to make good the shortfall on the *Princess Royal*. As the Mediterranean Pass, issued on 16th April 1789, only records that the ship was bound to Africa and the Americas, it is not possible to be more precise about the intended destination.[50]

4. Shipwreck and Slavery.

The maiden voyage of the *Anna*, Irving's first captaincy, began propitiously. As he sailed from Liverpool on 3rd May 1789, he wrote to his wife, Mary, informing her of the good progress made by the ship. He commented on the 'fine promising wind' which was 'so exceeding favourable the vessel runs out very fast...' The tone of the letter is calm and reassuring and was intended no doubt to relieve the anxieties his wife, two months pregnant at the time, felt about the voyage. He urged her not to 'fret and distress yourself without cause' but to trust in Providence who 'is able and willing to support you in every situation in life'. The demands placed upon Irving in his new position as captain, particularly on the first day of the venture, probably explain the brevity of this letter. It was with some regret that he told his wife that 'I really cannot find time to say what I have within...', although he did promise that 'the next I write shall be a very long one' (Letter 9).

James Irving did not, in fact, have the opportunity to write to his wife again until August 1789. In a letter dated the first of that month from 'Telling in Barbary' he informed her that, 'As a dream all our hopes and prospects are vanished. The *Anna* is wrecked and everything lost...' (Letter 16). It seems unlikely that she would have received this letter, conveyed from Morocco by James M. Matra, Consul General at Tangier, before September 1789. It was Matra who had informed the Secretary of State's office in London in a letter dated 21st July 1789 that the ship was 'wrecked on the Arab coast, opposite the west end of Fuertaventura' (Letter 13). Official confirmation of the loss of the *Anna* was not available in the shipping newspaper, *Lloyd's List*, until the 29th September 1789 when it was reported that 'The *Ann*, Irving, from Leverpool to Guinea, is wrecked at Uld Nun; the cargo plundered, and crew made slaves'. The same news was not reported in the local paper, *Williamson's Liverpool Advertiser*, until October 5th 1789 with the announcement that the ship was wrecked at 'Ohl Nun'. A navigational chart of 1794 indicates that 'Nun' was located on the north-western coast of Africa, opposite the Canary Islands and in present day maps it is recorded as 'Noun'(see Map 4).[1]

The events leading to the shipwreck are described in letters that Irving sent to consular officials in Morocco. In an appeal that he drafted to send to Matra some two months after the shipwreck he outlined that he was 'bound to the Gold Coast of Africa, but was carried on by a strong current and wrecked on the 27th May last ...'[2] Irving's journal, probably written some twelve or eighteen months after the events, provides a fuller account of the circumstances of the shipwreck. He records that the favourable wind that eased his passage from Liverpool was soon replaced by more inimical weather conditions and the progress of the ship was more halting. The journal creates a strong impression of the confusion that was felt about the ship's location as they approached the Canary Islands:[3]

Having duly considered our course, and the compass steered by since we last took our departure, there was a strong presumption of our being to the westward of Hegranza. In consequence of that opinion, she was steered south per compass with a view to make Lancerota or Fortaventura before night. However, 6 p.m. arrived without any appearance of either, although we had run 34 miles. Thus baffled in our expectations, we were unanimously of opinion that an easterly current during our run from the Burlings had deceived us, and that we were certainly to the eastward of the Canaries, however unaccountably it had happened. Fully persuaded thereof we hauled up S.W.B.W. till sunset (7 p.m.) distance run 7 miles, and although we were favoured with clear weather, could see no land from the masthead. We had then not a doubt of our being between the Canaries and the Barbary shore, and in order to avoid any probability of danger, steered W.S.W. till 11 p.m. when the atmosphere that had hitherto been clear, became a little cloudy and the breeze freshened.

This reference to an eastward current pulling the ship off course is remarkably similar to a passage in John Newton's diary during a voyage on the *Duke of Argyle*. An entry for Friday 21st September 1751 describes how:[4]

At 4 p.m. made the land right ahead, proved the island Grand Canaries; soon after saw the peak of Tenariff, W. $1/2$. S., a great distance, reckoned about 25 leagues ... By a good observation I find that my octant agrees very well with the latitude laid down in the tables in the Mariners' Compass. If the longitude in the charts and tables are anything near the truth, we must have come between Madera and Port Sancto, though think it strange that we saw neither. I am consequently not less than 50 leagues to the eastward of my reckoning, which as we have had constant fair winds and weather and frequent observations, must be owing to a strong current setting to the eastward, which cannot suppose less than 20 miles *per diem* from the time we passed the parallel of Cape St. Vincent or 37°.

The similarity of experience recorded by the two slave traders is interesting and reflects the dangers of the Barbary coast. In a map which forms a frontispiece to James Grey Jackson's early nineteenth century work, *An Account of the Empire of Morocco*, the coastal area around 'Noon' where the *Anna* was wrecked is marked with the notation that the 'current runs strong from hence towards the land which is extremely flat and the atmosphere hazy as far down as Cape Bajador in latitude 26:12 North'. Jackson cautioned that 'vessels bound to Senegal, the coast of Guinea, Sierra Leone, the Cape de Verde Islands should vigilantly watch the currents that invariably set in from the west towards this deceitful coast, which has in times past and now continues to enveigle ships to destruction'.[5]

If as these accounts suggest, the dangers were well-known, it seems surprising that Irving 'contrary to his inclinations...was ordered by his owners to sail between the Canaries and the coast of Africa ...' This suggestion that culpability for the shipwreck lay with John Dawson is contained in the published writings of William Lempriere who met Captain Irving during his captivity in Morocco.[6] Clearly, in the version of events that Irving related to this acquaintance he may have been trying to evade responsibility for what might be interpreted by others as poor seamanship.

The journal graphically describes the shipwreck of the *Anna*:

I had not left the deck above ten minutes, when I heard the man at the helm say the water looked comically. Much alarmed at the expression, I jumped on deck and was met by a heavy broken sea that fell on board. We instantly endeavoured to haul the sheets aft and bring her to the wind which blew fresh at North or N.B.W., but the breakers fell on board so heavily and followed one another so quickly, that she soon lost headway and struck in the hollow of the sea so very hard, that the rudder went away in a few seconds. She bounced with every wave so far to leeward that she lifted very little, but fell with such a shock that we expected every minute to find her part asunder or overset. In about ten minutes she filled, and the danger of over-setting being thereby increased we cut away the main-mast and hove everything of any weight that lay upon her deck overboard in order to prevent it. She lay for some time bow to sea, which considerably prevented her going to pieces.

The journal relates how the vessel 'lay buffetted by heavy breakers, already buildged, and full of water ...' The crew debated whether to abandon ship by means of a raft, but Irving records that they decided to stay on the *Anna* in the belief that the vessel would hold together until daylight. Daybreak presented to them a 'low, flat, white sandy shore at the distance of a cables length'. As there was only about four foot of water alongside, they waded ashore and viewed the scene and saw 'nothing but one uniform flat sand at high water, and rugged rocks at low water, bounded by a high breaker and heavy surf'. On examination of the ship they 'found her keel entirely beat off from stem to stern, two large holes in her starboard bilge, and her water way and starboard side opened'. As pointed out by Irving in the journal there was no hope of re-floating the vessel.

Also lost in the shipwreck was 'her cargo, India, Manchester and hardware goods with about 20 tons salt, which was washed out'. In a report of events to the British Vice-Consul in Mogodore, Irving pointed out that 'she had also 1,000 dollars on board, all of which fell into the hands of the Arabs' (Letters 10 and 11). This description of the cargo of the *Anna* is typical of the range of goods normally used to purchase slaves on the west coast of Africa. That the *Anna* was bound for Africa to purchase slaves is confirmed by a parliamentary listing of slave ship clearances for the years 1788 to 1792, a source that provides yet further confirmation that the vessel owned by John Dawson did not return to port.[7]

Shipwreck was not unusual. Other ships foundered on the journey to the west coast of Africa as the 'marine intelligence' in local newspapers readily attests. Even the crew's subsequent captivity, sale and enslavement is not exceptional as there are a number of accounts of seamen who suffered a similar fate. Other

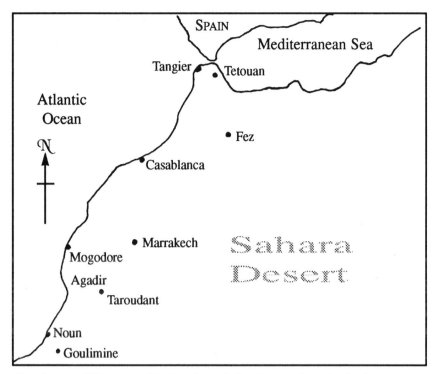

Sketch map of Morocco, showing the main locations referred to in the text.

seamen were sold into slavery following capture by Barbary corsairs.[8] It is, however, difficult to assess the frequency of enslavement on the Barbary coast in the eighteenth century resulting from shipwreck and the activities of privateers. James Grey Jackson estimated that in the period between 1790 and 1806, 30 ships of different nations were wrecked on the Barbary coast, suggesting an average of two ships per year. Of these, 17 were English vessels and he estimates that at least 120 crew members spent a period of captivity in Morocco and the Sahara desert, of whom 80 were eventually redeemed from slavery.[9] What distinguishes the shipwreck of the *Anna* from the normal type of nautical misadventure is that the crew of a ship heading to Africa to purchase slaves was captured and sold into slavery. Moreover, letters written by the captain provide a detailed record of his experiences in slavery, which is unusual as few accounts written by eighteenth century slave ship captains are known to survive.

By the time Captain James Irving wrote in a 'shameful scrawl done with a reed' to John Hutchison, British Vice-Consul in Mogodore, he had been in captivity for almost a month. In two letters, dated 24th June and 25th June 1789 written from 'Telling' in Barbary, Irving describes that since the shipwreck 'he and his crew, eleven in number inclusive, have been since that time in the hands of Arabs and Moors in a condition miserable beyond conception'(Letters 10 and 11). Separated from the other members of his crew, Irving pleaded with Hutchison to 'rescue us speedily from the most intollerable slavery'. Although he tries to contain his desperation within the boundaries and etiquette of formal address, he makes an emotive appeal in which he provides a brief synopsis of what had occurred since the shipwreck:[10]

> O I hope you can feel for us, first suffering shipwreck, then seized on by a party of Arabs with outstretched arms and knives ready to stab us, next stripped to the skin suffering a thousand deaths daily, insulted, spit upon, exposed to the sun and night dews alternally, then travelled through parched deserts wherein was no water for 9 days, afterwards torn from one another and your poor petitioner marched to this place half dead with fatigue, whose only hope is in God and you.

A fuller account of their capture is contained in the copy journal, the details of which are entirely consistent with letters that Irving wrote to Hutchison, the Vice-Consul, (Letters 10 and 11) and Matra, the Consul General. An entry for 28th May 1789 describes how:

> About ten o'clock in the forenoon perceived live animals at a great distance and soon after observed a flock of sheep, and almost at the same instant observed three people running from us over a small eminence that lay before us. We were all now big with anxiety, hopes, fears, resolutions and cowardice, a strange medley of ideas, some dropping astern, others pushing ahead. In this condition of mind three copper colored naked savages appeared before us on the top of the rising ground ahead of us, running at full speed and shouting hideously. They were followed by a tribe, some armed with long knives, others with muskets; you cannot conceive a scene more shocking, at least were you the victim on which it was practised. We were seized by the throats and our bundles instantly disappeared, as well as our neck handkerchiefs. They then cut and tore the clothes from our backs and so eager were they for the plunder that the weakest, who in all probability would get a small share of it, attempted to stab us. I for my own part was struck at with a large dagger several times, and must have been terribly mangled had not a strong man defended me till he got wounded in the arm; the assailant then sheathed his weapon, and was allowed share of the plunder. During this scene of rapine, had frequent opportunity of seeing my unfortunate shipmates served in the same manner, and fresh parties of Arabs coming from tents that lay at a greater distance

occasioned a repitition of the scene, several times, till we were stripped almost naked.

Few details are provided about their captors, but as Matra in later correspondence with the Secretary of State's office described them as 'wild Arabs' it suggests a nomadic rather than a sedentary tribe (Letter 13). As Europeans tended to use the description 'Arabs' loosely, it is difficult to be certain of the origins of the people with whom Irving came into contact. Irving's journal indicates that immediately after their capture the crew was taken to a 'dowhar' or village of tents that 'appeared at the distance of half a mile like mole hills in the sand' and the men were dispersed amongst a number of the characteristically low-lying, dark coloured tents in the encampment. In a later petition for help to Matra, Irving explained how they were 'detained amongst their tents 12 days' during which time they subsisted mainly on shellfish which they gathered from the shore.[11]

During the twelve day period from 28th May to 8th June 1789, Irving records that he had intermittent contact with a number of different crew members. It was 'one of the blacks' who informed him in the afternoon of 28th May that his second mate and apprentice were at another tent about 30 yards away. From a later entry of 31st May in which Irving refers to 'our three black people' it is clear that the earlier reference was to a crew member. This is confirmed by the crew list that Irving provided for Hutchison in his correspondence of 24th/25th June 1789. Silvin Buckle, James Drachen and Jack Peters are bracketed together as 'Portuguese blacks' in the letter which is amongst Foreign Office papers in the Public Record Office. Most of the eleven crew members are mentioned by name in later sections of the journal; names which correspond with those listed in Irving's letter of 25th June 1789. These names are also consistent with a further listing that Matra sent to the Secretary of State's office in December 1789.[12] As no muster roll exists for the *Anna*, this is indeed impressive evidence to confirm the authenticity of the journal.

One of Irving's principal concerns throughout his period in captivity was the welfare of his cousin, James Irving II, who sailed on the *Anna* as ship's surgeon. In a journal entry for 29th May Captain Irving records his 'infinite satisfaction' when he observed his 'mate and cousin coming from three of four tents about a quarter of a mile distant'. One of the men had 'been cut in the thigh when his pocket was cut off' during the previous day's struggle, although both retained a flannel shirt and trousers. The list that Irving later supplied to Hutchison indicates that John Clegg was the first mate of the *Anna*, an individual who had sailed with Irving on previous slave voyages on board the *Jane*. The same list indicates that M. Francis Dawson, a 'nephew of the merchant's' was the second mate with whom Irving had been reunited the previous day (Letter 10).

Irving records that they agreed to use their 'joint endeavours to keep together and share the same fate' which they recognised would probably be one of slavery. In an entry for 2nd June, Irving describes the struggle which ensued when an attempt was made 'by the man who claims me as his property' to separate him from the other members of the crew. Irving, knocked to the ground by several blows, resisted by clinging to his companions as he 'would rather have parted with life, than have been taken away alone'. Despite assurances not to separate them, the second mate and apprentice were taken away in the afternoon leaving Captain Irving, his cousin and chief mate alone. It appears that by this point all the other members of the crew had been dispersed for sale and it was these three remaining officers who on June 8th were 'marched in 9 days more through barren parched desarts and mountaneous wilds' to the village of 'Guilemene' (Goulimine as it appears on present day maps).[13]

The journey to Goulimine, a settlement that lies on the edge of the Sahara about forty miles to the south-east of the location of their shipwreck at Noun, was arduous (see Map 4). The walking conditions in parts must have been extremely difficult as an entry for 9th June records how they 'passed over several hills of accumulated sand that kept blowing before the wind like snow'. On a number of occasions he was 'indulged' with a ride on one of the six camels in the caravan and found that it was a 'most uneasy animal, but as we were exceedingly fatigued made a shift to hang on them for an hour or two...'. Added to the difficulties of the terrain that they had to traverse, he noted that the 'heat and drought was so intense, that the hills and valleys were like parched ashes'. The river beds over which they passed were typically dried up, water was in short supply and Irving describes how some of their convoy obtained brackish water by digging a hole in the sand. After the first day of travelling Irving records that the three officers 'craved a drink of water' but they were obliged to 'drink it out of our hats, as the dish would have been polluted had any of us touched it with our lips'. The next day they were given an old wooden dish from which to eat as 'the people in every place would never again have used a dish that we had eat or drank out of, so great was their detestation and contempt of us'. Their captors were undoubtedly Sunni Muslims, the predominant religious group in eighteenth century Morocco, and their actions reflect the widespread and deep rooted hostility to Christians.[14]

By June 12th Irving records that he was 'scarcely able to walk with fatigue and despondency', and the events of the following days only added to his sense of despair. An occurrence of June 15th seems to have particularly disturbed him. He was given a pair of scissors to cut his beard which 'was by this time very long and troublesome' and 'that action as it too much resembled the practice followed by slave traders gave us much trouble'.

Following their arrival at Goulimine on 16th June 1789, Irving was separated from his cousin and chief mate, indicating that they had been sold to different masters. Captain Irving was housed with an individual named Bilade who had escorted them in the latter part of the journey to Goulimine, whilst his cousin and chief mate were taken to the king 'who he called Muley Abderhaman'. According to this account in the copy journal some of the crew were already with 'Prince Muley Abderhaman' (more correctly written as Mawlay 'Abd. al-Rahman), who was an exiled son of Sidi Muhammad b. 'Abd. Allah, Emperor of Morocco.[15] This information is consistent with the account that Irving supplied to Hutchison in his first letter of 24th June (Letter 10). Clearly isolated from the others, he informed the Vice-Consul that 'my mate, surgeon and six men are with the Muley Abdrahman at Gulimeme, working while the sun shines in the open field'. He was unsure of the location of the remaining two crew members, his second mate and apprentice, not having seen or heard of them since they were taken away on 2nd June 1789.

Irving spent just under a week at Goulimine, and the account in the copy journal relates that much of this time was spent 'in a most melancholy distracted state of mind, employed carrying water for the cattle etc.'. He described Goulimine in the following terms:

It appears at a little distance like a fortification, as does every village in Barbary. The place we saw in the forenoon was another village of the same kind. They consist of a number of houses built of clay and closely connected with one another, so that the outside houses appear like the bastions and curtains of a fortified town. They are flat at the top with a battlement around them, appearing at a short distance like ambrazures.

It is estimated that in the early nineteenth century Goulimine, a passage or focus for the movement of Saharan caravans, had a population of about 800 people.[16] Although Irving described Goulimine as a village, it is probable that a settlement of this size in the context of the dispersed rural population of the Saharan provinces was regarded as a town by contemporaries. The urban population of late eighteenth century Morocco was small, accounting for between 5 and 10 per cent of a population of four to five million.[17] James Grey Jackson described Goulimine, also known as Wedinoon as 'a kind of intermediate depot for merchandise on its way to Soudan, and for the produce of Soudan going to Mogodor'.[18]

Irving was sold a second time at Goulimine. In an entry in the journal for July 1789 he records that 'About this time I was informed ... that I had been bought from Bilade at Gulimene by Sheik Brahim, my present master, for a hundred and thirty five ducats'. This corresponds with Matra's report to Whitehall of 7th

August 1789 that Irving 'is a few miles from Muly Abderhamen, with a master who gave 135 dollars for him...'[19] As a result of this further sale, Irving was taken from Goulimine on 22nd June by a party which 'consisted of about a dozen, mounted on horses'. Irving's account of the journey suggests that they travelled in a north-easterly direction through mountainous countryside, parts of which were cultivated and populous.

By 24th June, the date of his first letter to Hutchison, Irving was at a place called 'Teilin'. In the journal he records that:

> at the close of day we got to Telling, my master's residence. Here were about 12 families of Jews, who were under my master's protection. At the house of one of them, a fowl was boiled for me, and he told me in broken Spanish (of which I understood a little) that I must reside with him at my master's expense.

Variously spelt by Irving as 'Telling', 'Teilin' and 'Tellin', this was probably a very small settlement as it is not marked on contemporary or modern day maps. In a letter to his wife dated 1st August 1789, he indicated that his crew at Goulimine was 'about 30 miles from this place' (Letter 16). In a journal entry of 30th November 1789, Irving records that he was a three day journey from Taroudant. Taken together, the various references suggest that 'Telling' lay about 30 miles north-east of Goulimine, close to the coastal end of the Anti-Atlas mountain range (see Map 4).

The arrival, at 'Telling' represented a new phase in Irving's already long period of captivity. The events of the following two days offered Irving some new hope for freedom, yet at the same time highlighted the fragility of this hope. Irving's journal records the despair which he experienced as a result of a meeting on 24th June with the crew of a French ship that had been wrecked off the same coastline on 2nd or 3rd January 1789. Irving was informed that their vessel, heading for Senegal 'with a cargo suited for the gum trade' was 'bilged, but that the natives gathered round them in great numbers, so that they had voluntarily surrendered'. These seamen had been set to work in the fields and despite repeated pleas to their consul at Sale there was no immediate prospect of release. It was this information that dismayed Irving:

> This intelligence almost petrified me with misery. I could have died rather than devote my life to be spent in so abject a state, bereft of all Christian society, a slave to a savage race who despised and hated me for my belief.

If this information diminished Irving's faith in the diplomatic process, he still took full advantage of the opportunity that was offered later that day and the following day to write to John Hutchison, British Vice-Consul at Mogodore. He was instructed to inform Hutchison of his 'misfortune and situation' as he was assured that the Vice-Consul would 'send and purchase me, and that myself and crew (if alive) would be returned to our native country'. Irving records that 'this intelligence quickened the small degree of hope that remained...'.[20]

The entry in the journal for 25th June is entirely consistent with the contents of the surviving letters in Foreign Office papers, even down to the details of the implement used for writing (Letters 10 and 11). Irving describes that he 'wrote with a reed on coarse wrapping paper a long and plaintive letter to the Consul and enclosed a list of the vessel's crew as they stood on the articles, requesting at the same time that he would take the earliest opportunity to inform Mr. Dawson of the fate of the *Anna*, his vessel'. Irving's meeting with the Frenchmen influenced the content of the letter as he urges the Vice-Consul 'Suffer us not any longer like some poor Frenchmen about 10 or 12 miles from hence to be the slaves of Negroes...'. In a comment on the French Consul, Irving depicts the continued enslavement of the French crew as a sign of 'negligence on the man who should see them liberated'. In later correspondence it is apparent that the release of the French crew became very closely linked to the negotiations for the crew of the *Anna*.

Although Sheik Brahim's probable motive for purchasing Irving was to make a profit by ransoming him to interested parties, it is clear that he threatened the captain with a life of slavery in the agrarian economy of Morocco. In a letter dated 25th June 1789 Irving informs Hutchison that 'the people here tell me if you do not pay for me or get me released, in ten days I go out to the fields to work at the corn. This you'll acknowledge to be hard. I was bred a surgeon originally, and God knows how I shall endure it'. The letter, an outpouring of emotions built up over the previous month of captivity, reflects Irving's underlying fear that 'if we are allowed to stay here to toil and be maltreated under a vertical sun we shall soon be lost forever to ourselves, our wives and familys, our country and all we hold dear' (Letter 10).

On a more practical level, Irving informs Hutchison of the people who would stand as surety for any sum that was expended on their behalf in ransom money. He assured Hutchison that 'our merchants are very affluent and some of us have friends that would be happy in having an opportunity to prove themselves such.' In addition to his two uncles in London, Captain Anthony Robinson and Mr. Joseph Smith, Irving lists the merchant John Dawson and William Sherwood, a captain in the slave trade, as people who would be his 'vouchers in this melancholy business ...' In the initial part of the letter Irving assumed that their ransom would be similar to the sum demanded for the Frenchman of one hundred dollars each. In a later section of the letter though he records that 'I am at this moment told that 500 dollars per man is the sum expected'. Consequently, he offered to stand security for just himself and his cousin, although by the final paragraph of the letter he had extended this to include Matthew Dawson, the nephew of his employer. He points out that he cannot afford to redeem the chief mate and other crew members as 'I have not the sum ...' In a revealing comment he informs Hutchison that 'if your goodness extends itself towards them, the whites particularly, I am almost certain restitution will be quickly made'.

The perplexity that Irving felt emerges powerfully from the letters of 24th and 25th June, and is succinctly conveyed in the final question that he directs to Hutchison in which he points out 'We are not on hostile terms with the Moors, and I have a pass granted by the Lords Commissioners of the Admiralty, therefore why are we detained my good Sir?'. The Mediterranean Pass to which Irving refers was issued to protect shipping from 'capture or plunder by the Barbary pirates operating off the Atlantic as well as the Mediterranean coast of North West Africa'.[21] The pass, which Irving had 'concealed in the headband of my drawers, unknown to my tyrannical proprietors', furnished the crew of the *Anna* with no meaningful protection from the nomadic desert tribes. Some importance was still attached to it though as Hutchison, in a letter written in July 1789, points out that 'I have received the pass safe, and it shall be transmitted to the Admiralty Office in order that the bond for it may be cancelled' and that 'I will take care in due time to furnish you with my official receipt for it' (Letter 14). The register of passes does indeed record that pass number 7469 issued to James Irving, master of the *Anna*, at Liverpool on 16th April 1789 was returned on 24th August 1789.[22]

This contact that Irving established with Hutchison almost a month after the shipwreck did represent a positive change in his circumstances. The regular correspondence which ensued meant that Irving had a point of contact to meliorate his sense of isolation and a safety valve for his obvious frustration. Although Hutchison's early replies to Irving could offer little substantive hope of immediate change, he was able at least to offer some rational explanation for his situation. In a letter dated 10th July 1789, Hutchison pointed out that securing their freedom was more complex than Irving had supposed as '... no money I could offer, and would chearfully advance, can effect the purpose without the intervention of the Emperor, who will be very soon informed concerning you' (Letter 12).

The situation was more complex still, as Irving and his crew had been shipwrecked in an area that was outside the formal control of the Emperor of Morocco. With limited military resources and bureaucratic structures, the Makhzan or Moroccan state was unable to extend effective control over the southern Saharan provinces in the eighteenth and early nineteenth centuries. Sultan Muhammad III showed little interest in trying to pacify these areas, but concentrated on his northern provinces and the encouragement of trade with

Europe. As the historian El Mansour points out the southern territories, remote and inaccessible, remained largely independent and were regarded as 'zones of dissidence'.[23] Moreover, as Matra explained to the Secretary of State's office most of the seamen were 'in the hands of Muly Abderhaman, an excommunicated son of the Emperor (his second) who remains independent of his father, and is maintained by the free Arabs'. Although Matra intended to apply to Court for their release he expressed his 'doubts of immediate success' in a letter of 21st July 1789. In this letter, one of his regular reports to Whitehall, Matra anticipated the difficulties of negotiation as 'the Prince will listen to no terms from his father on any occasion, and I am afraid that the Emperor will not readily consent to let anybody treat with his son' (Letter 13). El Mansour's study of Morocco in the late eighteenth century and early nineteenth century indicates that Mawlay 'Abd. al-Rahman was the leading political figure who controlled the territory around Goulimine until the area was pacified in 1807, albeit temporarily by Mawlay Sulayman, his younger brother.[24]

The replies that Hutchison sent to Irving, a large number of which survive amongst the collection in the Lancashire Record Office, indicate that Irving wrote to him time and time again to establish whether any progress had been made in the negotiations for his release. These letters, together with the record of proceedings contained in Matra's official correspondence, indicate the two-pronged approach of diplomacy. Firstly, a sustained effort was made to improve the men's situation whilst in captivity. Secondly, a number of devices was used by Hutchison and Matra to secure the release of Irving and his crew which took full account of the complex political circumstances in Morocco. This combined approach is effectively conveyed by Hutchison in a letter of mid/late July 1789 in which he tells Irving that 'it will give me the utmost pleasure to contribute to your ease and comfort whilst under restraint, and to your deliverance as soon as possible' (Letter 14).

The month of August, Irving's third in captivity, saw only the most marginal progress in negotiations for release. For Irving the time spent in captivity passed extremely slowly, and he clearly detested his work as a servant to Aaron Debauny, the Jew with whom he had been lodged. He described the work as 'most meanly servile' and found it all the more difficult to accept as he was aware of the inferior ('dhimma') status of Jews in Moroccan society.[25] In a letter to Hutchison dated 2nd August 1789 Irving recorded that 'the prospect darkens as the time lengthens'. He describes how 'the state of quiet and serenity that I boasted of and thought had attained is almost wore away, and two packets arriving within these few days without any letter or good news, depressed me still more' (Letter 17). In contrast, the weight of diplomatic inertia was such that Matra in a letter to the Secretary of State's office dated 7th August 1789 dispassionately commented that 'it is not yet time to hear what has been done towards the relief of our men in the hands of the Arabs'.[26]

Irving's anxiety and 'great unhappiness' was also related to the reports he had received from his men of the material deprivation and gratuitous cruelty to which they claimed they were subjected. He refers to a letter which he received from his men at the end of July in which 'they write in bad spirits' (Letter 17). This is again consistent with an entry in the journal in which he records that he 'received a letter from my officers and people, in which they complained pitifully of the usage they received. They were beat most unmercifully and toiled hard from sunrise to sunset...'. In the letter to Hutchison of 2nd August Irving related the details of his crew's experiences:

> Their master...most certainly intends to free them from their distresses by being their murderer. They say that when they are struggling under their burdens and exerting their utmost strength to accomplish their tasks, that he beats them most unmercifully and stands by till his Negroes beat them with sticks. One of them has an abscess in his hand that has penetrated through amongst the sinnews on the back of it and the surgeon is sick, his ailment is not mentioned. Yet notwithstanding, the same duty is expected from them, they must work if they die under their load. They also say that they scarcely obtain provision enough to sustain life. They had saved by some means or other 7 or 8 dollars, and one day being impelled by hunger offered one for anything that was eatable. As soon as he was informed thereof he ordered them to be stripped and searched, he found and took them from them. They also write me that 2 of the 6 pairs of shoes that where sent them, he hath taken and put on the feet of his own Negroes while they go barefooted, an action that would degrade a peasant, nay a highwayman, yet he deems it meritorious as he laughed heartily at it.

Hutchison responded promptly to Irving's letter of the 2nd August as 'the contents very much affect me, both on your account and that of your people, who, I am sorry to see are so inhumanely treated'. In this letter dated 13th August he again reassured Irving of his 'best endeavours' and reported to him the steps that had been taken towards their 'deliverance' (Letter 18). Hutchison agreed to pay the ransom demanded by Sheik Brahim, the terms of which Irving had been instructed to set out in his letter of 2nd August. The total price demanded for nine of the crew members was 1,200 dollars. One quarter of this, 300 dollars, was the price that was set for Captain Irving and one of the black seamen, James Drachen, who had recently been purchased at Goulimine and taken to 'Telling' by Sheik Brahim. The remaining 900 dollars was for seven men with Mawlay 'Abd. al-Rahman, which included the chief mate, the surgeon, three white seamen and two Portuguese blacks.

Hutchison appeared optimistic that by negotiating directly with Sheik Brahim, he could secure the release of the seamen. However, further delays ensued. According to the entries in the copy journal for August 1789, Sheik Brahim rejected Hutchison's offer and attempted to improve his bargaining position by purchasing three more seamen from Mawlay 'Abd. al-Rahman:

> But he, instead of accepting his offer, collected all the money he could and went in two or three days afterwards to Gulimene, in order to purchase as many of the others as his purse would effect. In a week he returned with William Brown, John Richards and Jack Peters, three others of the crew, and desired me to write the Consul that our prices were now augmented to nine hundred dollars for the five in his possession, and Muley Abderhaman would not take less for the four with him, than seven hundred dollars.

Irving records that this news 'afforded fresh cause of grief and misery to us', as they were fearful that their prices might be increased yet again.

Further complications arose from the fact that Hutchison did not have the power to act completely independently, as any offer to Sheik Brahim had to be made in the context of imperial approval. The Vice-Consul clearly thought that he possessed this when he wrote to Irving on 13th August:

> The Emperor being informed of your misfortune, gave immediate orders to a Jew (Sintop Ben Attar) to send and purchase you at any price. The Jew is willing, but has not the power. I have wrote him to offer him every assistance in my power, and that I will be answerable for any difference there may be betwixt the Emperor's allowance and your real ransom (Letter 18).

A fortnight later, though, Hutchison explained to Irving 'there has intervened some small obstacle...' which meant that he no longer had the authorisation to act. He explained that:

> When I wrote you and made the proposition to Sheak Braham it was, as you will see by my letter, in the intelligence that a Jew, Sintop Ben Attar, was commissioned by the Emperor to purchase you. My interference was, consequently, under his supposed sanction. The Jew arrived here and informed me that it was true the Emperor had given him such orders, but had immediately withdrawn them and desired his son, Muley Absolem to do it. I was consequently obliged to stop farther proceedings till I am authorised either by the Emperor or the Prince, who is now at Tarrudant (Letter 19).

In Matra's opinion, Sultan Muhammad III's actions were calculated and deliberately intended to secure a favour from the British consulate. In a letter of 5th September Matra concisely explained to his correspondent that the Emperor 'has since recalled the Jew and given his power to Prince Abslem, I suspect to induce me to get a doctor for Abslem' as 'the Emperor is very desirous to have an English occulist to attend his son, who is almost blind'. From this point, 'Prince Muley Absolem' (Mawlay 'Abd. al Salam) became a key figure in the negotiations for the release of the crew of the *Anna*. Judging from this letter of 5th September Matra had already decided to send for a doctor from Gibraltar to attend the Prince. Matra clearly viewed this course of action as judicious, as he commented that 'I dare say I shall get the people soon, perhaps cheaper, for I have many irons in the fire, but the doctor I hold to be the best'.[27]

The first doctor selected for this task refused to leave Gibraltar as he was 'frightened by some medling people in the garrison...'[28] By 24th September though, Matra informed William Wyndham Grenville, Secretary of State for the Home Department, that he had 'at last procured a good doctor for the Prince, who goes tomorrow for Mogodore, a favour that will make him zealous to procure the seamen, and most probably induce him to be useful to me at Court'.[29] Three days later, Matra informed Irving of this new development and pointed out that it was 'a place that I certainly would not have risked a subject in were it not for the prospect of being useful to you and your people' (Letter 21).

The doctor, William Lempriere, arrived in Morocco on 14th September 1789. The account that he subsequently wrote of his travels is well-known to students of late eighteenth century Morocco. It contains an intriguing mix of factual observation and highly descriptive accounts of his encounters and experiences. In the introductory section he describes how he was promised a 'liberal reward for his professional exertions' by Mawlay 'Abd. al Salam and that he would be free to leave the country as soon as he was required by his garrison in Gibraltar. Lempriere records though:[30]

> ... the most flattering circumstance which attended this requisition of the Moorish prince was the release of certain Christian captives who were at this period detained in slavery. These unfortunate persons consisted of the master of an English vessel trading to Africa, and nine seamen, who had been wrecked upon that part of the coast which is inhabited by the wild Arabs, and were carried into slavery by that savage and merciless people.

Lempriere spent two weeks with Matra at Tangier before being summoned to attend to his patient at Taroudant, the Prince's usual residence (see Map 4). He reached Taroudant late in the month of October 1789 and notes that two hours before his arrival that 'the whole of the English people who had been shipwrecked, except the Captain and a Negro, passed through the town in their way to the metropolis'.[31]

James Drachen, a Portuguese black, was the man left in captivity with Irving. The copy journal records that after William Brown, John Richards and Jack

Peters were 'redeemed and taken away by some officers of the Emperor' early in October 1789, 'the poor man felt the separation so sensibly that in two days afterwards he sickened and in twelve days more, paid the debt of nature'. A report later written by Matra confirms that it was James Drachen who died in captivity, as his is the only name missing from a crew list that the Consul General sent to Whitehall in December 1789.[32]

Captain Irving, therefore, spent the month of November isolated from the rest of his crew. The copy journal records that he suffered a recurrence of the fever that had so debilitated him during the month of September. He clearly had not fully recovered from the earlier attack which daily rendered him 'delirious during the hot stage of the paroxism'. His illness in late October and November was sufficiently severe to halt the flow of his regular correspondence with Hutchison and it appears that the Vice-Consul had expressed some concern about Irving's well-being. In a letter addressed to William Wyndham Grenville dated 19th December 1789 Matra points out that.[33]

By Mr. Hutchison's last letters he still continues uneasy on the Captain's account whom he had not heard from for a long time; but Doctor Lempriere in a letter to me of the 24 hour, says Prince Abslem that morning had sent off a party to bring in Captain Irving, which makes me hope they have certain intelligence of his being alive.

Irving's journal records that on 30th November 'three horsemen belonging to Prince Absolam ... arrived at the house of my master, and with much difficulty purchased me for two hundred dollars'. After a journey in which Irving was still clearly suffering from the effects of his illness, they reached Taroudant on 3rd December 1789. The journal records that on his arrival Mawlay 'Abd. al-Salam sought Irving's advice on his complaint and in subsequent weeks required the surgeon to visit him on a daily basis. As Matra points out in an informal letter to Evan Nepean, a government administrator whom he treated as a confidant, Irving 'having been bred a surgeon, he detains with him till he departs for Court'.[34]

It was Lempriere who had informed Mawlay 'Abd. al-Salam that Captain Irving was a surgeon which 'he did to induce the Prince to send and redeem me, in order that I might attend him while the other was absent'. Other than mentioning that the Prince had a 'defect of sight', Irving says little of the nature of his complaint. Lempriere, in contrast, provides full details of the Prince's condition:[35]

I have already intimated that the Prince had totally lost the use of one eye by a cataract; and I may add, that he had nearly lost that of the other by a paralytic affection, which threatened to end in a gutta serena (By this disease is to be understood, such a state of the optic nerve as renders it insensible to the rays of light), and which had drawn the eye so much towards the nose, as sometimes entirely to exclude the appearance of the pupil. The only remains of sight left, were merely sufficient to enable him to see large bodies, without distinguishing any of them particularly. The spasm was the disease which I was ordered to cure.

Lempriere noted that after several weeks there was some improvement in the Prince's eyesight so that 'he could now distinguish an apple at about ten yards distance'. After a period of five weeks though, Lempriere was summoned to the court of the Emperor of Morocco, Muhammad III, and from the account it is clear that he left Taroudant before Captain Irving's arrival on 3rd December 1789.[36] As Irving does not provide a detailed account of the three week period spent at Taroudant, it is difficult to know whether he effected any improvement in the Prince's condition.

In common with Lempriere, Irving found the period at Taroudant demanding and frustrating. Both surgeons record that when it became generally known that they were doctors they were overwhelmed by the numbers of people wanting medical advice.[37] In a journal entry for December 1789 Irving records that 'during this time I was most grievously harassed by the uncivilised Moors who, hearing that I was a doctor, flocked around me in the streets and with outstretched hands begged I would examine their pulses, and so great was their ignorance, that they believed I could by so doing not only discover their complaints, but cure them'.[38]

Irving spent just over three weeks at Taroudant, which he described as a 'walled town of tolerable extent situated in the centre of a fruitful valley, well watered by a large river' and he noted that there 'are many fine gardens and a royal palace'. Some years later James Grey Jackson described Taroudant as the 'metropolis of the South', a reference to the fact that it was the centre for the state's administration of south-west Morocco. He noted that the town 'is spacious and very ancient' and that 'the buildings, generally speaking, are handsome'. The town, located on the river Sous, was set in fertile plains and was noted for the manufacture of leather goods.[39]

Irving left Taroudant, according to the entries in the copy journal, on 26th December 1789. As the Prince had been ordered to the city of Morocco (Marrakech) by the Emperor, Irving formed part of his caravan 'in number about three hundred, all mounted on horses, camels and mules'. The caravan reached the outside of the city walls at 3 p.m. on 31st December and Irving recorded in the journal that 'the surgeon who had been at Tarradant' was stood there waiting to 'pay his court to the Prince'. Lempriere describes their meeting:[40]

The Prince had brought along with him to Morocco, the English captain, the only Englishman that had been left in slavery, the black having died some time before. My reader will easily conceive the pleasure I felt at seeing my unfortunate countryman, who had been left alone in the hands of savages, now out of immediate slavery, and with the cheerful prospect, according to the promises of the Prince, of being immediately sent home to his friends and country. My sensations indeed on the occasion may be much more easily felt than described. But if this circumstance had such an effect upon me, what must it have had upon this unfortunate officer, who for some months past had been separated from his people, one of whom was a near relation, and without knowing whether they were dead or alive; who with the evils of slavery had experienced that of a severe fever, without having any person to console him, or afford him that assistance which is so necessary upon such occasions. To be redeemed under such circumstances from his inhospitable situation, to recover from his illness, and to meet with all his companions at Morocco, well taken care of by the Emperor, was a change which he had given up all expectation of ever beholding.

Irving's meeting with Lempriere and his reunion with his men took place at the city of Morocco (Marrakech) on New Year's Eve 1789. He records in his journal that he obtained permission to go 'with the surgeon and the others to their lodgings' and that 'the greatest part of the night was spent in reciting our hardships past and present'. It appears that Irving and Lempriere became more closely acquainted in the time spent at Morocco (Marrakech). Lempriere recorded that 'the captain was a well-informed young man, and an agreeable companion' and that his 'good sense and agreeable conversation lessened in great degree the uneasiness I experienced from the irksomeness of my situation...'[41]

In his *Tour* Lempriere shows some knowledge of Irving's background and a very detailed awareness of events surrounding the shipwreck and capture, and in many respects the account resembles that portrayed in the journal.[42] The later description that James Grey Jackson provides of the shipwreck and capture of sailors on the Barbary coast is very similar in outline to James Irving's experiences.[43] This is not surprising though, as Jackson had read Lempriere's work and was also closely acquainted with Matra, the Consul General, and Layton, a merchant in Mogodore, both of whom were actively involved in negotiating for the release of Captain Irving and his crew in 1789-90.[44]

During the weeks spent at Morocco (Marrakech), Irving re-established contact with Hutchison, the Vice-Consul. This had lapsed during late November and December due to Irving's 'malignant fever' and his move to Taroudant, of which

Hutchison seemed temporarily unaware.[45] By late December 1789, Hutchison had obviously received news that Irving was travelling to Morocco with Mawlay 'Abd. al-Salam as he sent a courier with a letter to meet him outside the city walls. Although this letter does not survive, Irving's journal records that Hutchison had made arrangements, through this courier, to supply him with clothes when he reached the city. Hutchison was clearly trying to spare Irving the indignity that his men had experienced when they had arrived at Morocco 'perfectly naked'.[46] In his journal for the 1st January 1790 Irving records:

> I received my parcel from the Moor that had been sent me from the Vice Consul. On opening it I found a complete suit of common clothes, and amongst the rest one of my own shirts that had been carried from the wreck and sold at Mogodore to the Vice Consul. He knew it, therefore purchased and sent it to me.

Although Hutchison had made every effort to supply Irving and his crew with clothing whilst they were in captivity in the southern provinces, his endeavours were frustrated by two main problems. The Vice-Consul had informed Irving as early as July 1789 that 'you may be assured that every necessary should be sent you were it not that any superfluity would be either stole or taken from you, or that any superior appearance would only tend to augment the difficulties of your redemption' (Letter 14). After shoes had been taken from Irving's men in captivity in Goulimine, Hutchison pointed out on 13th August 1789 that 'you see ... how useless it would be to send any superfluities...' (Letter 18). Consequently, Hutchison used presents of clothing and tea and sugar to encourage Irving's master, Sheik Brahim, to 'mend his behaviour'. Hutchison expressed satisfaction on 28th August 1789 that 'your master was pleased with his cloak, and that you felt some good effects from it' (Letter 19). The letters which Hutchison sent to Irving whilst he was in captivity in 'Telling' reveal that constant cajoling was necessary to retain Sheik Brahim's 'good offices'.

Hutchison was not constrained by such factors when the men reached Morocco (Marrakech), and he clearly felt freer to supply Irving and his crew with a sum of money that they used to support themselves. Hutchison urged Irving to inform him should they need anything 'as you will always find me ready and willing to supply whatever may be necessary for yourself or people' (Letter 25).

As much as Hutchison could contribute to the men's comfort, they were still not free to return to England. In his letter of 11th January 1790 Hutchison explained that 'All our hopes at present center in what Mr. Lempriere may be able to effectuate by means of Muley Absolem' (Letter 25). Lempriere had already achieved a great deal. In a letter of 27th December 1789, Matra explained to Evan Nepean that 'had he not been sent, the Prince would never have taken so much pain to procure Irving's men, as he has done, they would probably have remained in slavery till they expired; for the French who by the same opportunity got relieved, had been there near a twelve month before them'.[47] According to the surgeon's recollections in his *Tour*, the Prince assured him in the first week of January 1790 that he 'had succeeded to his wishes with the Emperor in what he had promised relative to the English captives'. Lempriere communicated this prospect of freedom to Captain Irving but 'he seemed too much accustomed to disappointments to entertain any very sanguine expectations from my information'. In subsequent days, however, the Prince left Morocco without taking the surgeon or the seamen with him as he had earlier promised. Lempriere records that:[48]

> ... in return for all the fatigues and inconveniences which I had experienced on his account, I found myself deserted entirely, and left in the charge of a haughty and perfidious Emperor. Doubt after doubt took possession of my mind, and this, joined with the reflection of having so completely disappointed the hopes of the unfortunate seamen, as well as the favourable accounts I had written to the Consul on the Prince's recovery, pressed so forcibly on my feelings, that for the space of two or three hours I was in a state little better than that of insanity.

Judging by a letter from Hutchison dated 18th January 1790 their release was not imminent as he referred to their being 'condemned to stay in the country for sometime longer...' (Letter 26). Although the long-term aim of diplomatic endeavour was to secure the release of the men, in the short-term Matra concentrated on having them transferred to Mogodore 'to remain with the Christians, where from the number of their countrymen they will be more comfortable; and as that town is well fortified by land, much safer from the first effects of a commotion in case of a revolt in the country'.

By the end of January Matra's objective had been secured, as on the 31st of that month Irving wrote to his wife and informed her that they had all reached Mogodore in 'perfect health'. At Mogodore they were put directly under John Hutchison's care and he supplied them with clothes and 'the necessarys of life...' (Letter 27). In the journal Irving records how Hutchison 'also procured a room for us'. Matra had insisted that they should all be lodged together so that the seamen 'may be under their officers observation...'. Matra was apparently relieved that the crew had been moved from Morocco (Marrakech) to Mogodore as:[49]

> ... the common men as usual were at times very intemperate, and as His Imperial Majesty affects to dislike drunkeness more than any other vice, there

would not have been much difficulty in prevailing on him to remove a bad example, and have the men sent home in a manner very expensive to us.

Mogodore (or Essaouira to use the Arabic name) was founded in 1764 by the Emperor, Muhammad III, to encourage foreign trade and to boost revenue for the Moroccan state. Set in a rather desolate, windswept position it was a planned settlement with a geometric plan, imposing gateways and bastions and a style quite out of character with other urban centres in Morocco.[50] The town, which remained the most important maritime centre in Morocco until the late nineteenth century, was described by Lempriere as:[51]

> ... a large uniform and well built town, situated about 350 miles from Tangier on the Atlantic ocean and surrounded on the landside by deep and heavy sands ... The entrance, both by sea and land, consists of elegant stone archways with double gates. The market place is handsomely built with piazzas of the same materials, and at the water port there is a custom house and powder magazine, both of which are neat stone buildings. Besides these public edifices, the Emperor has a small but handsome palace for his occasional residence. The streets of the town, though very narrow, are all in strait lines and the houses, contrary to what we meet with in the other towns of the Empire, are lofty and regular.

The first letter that Captain Irving wrote to his wife Mary from Mogodore on 31st January 1790 was genuinely buoyant and optimistic. Entering his ninth month of captivity, he entertained real hopes of freedom. Even though he was desperate to know how Mary had 'withstood the storm of fate' he advised her that 'as I have every prospect of being soon with you I think it will be improper to write now'. There is the impression that he thought his 'trial' was over and that he would soon return to England 'to enjoy the smiles of fortune once more'. In reflective mood, he pointed out:

> She hath jilted me once, but you know she's fickle and may next time be propitious. Let us be virtuous and Providence will uphold, as whom he loveth he chastiseth and afflicteth in order to render them worthy of his future care. Be cheerfull and repine not, my conduct will bear any scrutiny however severe and we shall flourish the more after our pruning.

In the same letter Captain Irving described Mogodore as a 'most hospitable place' as the European merchants 'strive who to outdo each other in kindness and hospitality' (Letter 27). Lempriere indicates that there were 'about a dozen mercantile houses of different nations...' in Mogodore, a figure that is regarded as reliable by recent writers.[52] Irving's younger cousin and namesake painted a similar picture of Mogodore when he wrote to his parents in Langholm on 25th

March 1790 to reassure them of his well being:

> ... we are now in a town where there are Christian merchants and shipping of different nations, which are very kind to me and we live very well. Have a house to ourselves, got good cloaths and [?]alwise money in our pockets and nothing to do but amuse ourselves so that we are just as well as we could wish only loosing our time (Letter 28).

In a letter written to Mary Irving on the following day, Captain Irving also pointed out that 'our distress is now only mental which we endeavour to lighten as much as possible by reading and other amusements'. Although he was still the Emperor's property, Irving pointed out that he had 'little reason to call myself a slave, but rather a prisoner at large...'. His movements, as well as those of his men, were largely unrestrained but the letter written at the end of March 1790 still conveys his tremendous anxiety and frustration (Letter 29). In this, as in a number of his later letters, there is an emotional tension between his attempts to comfort and reassure his wife and his overwhelming despondency. In his journal he obviously felt more at ease to record his true feelings:

> Our situation now may appear to many as tolerably comfortable, but when they are informed that the room we lodged in was no better than a cellar without a window or any kind of furniture. The ground made our bed, and we covered ourselves with a kind of blanket called a haique, one being given to each of us by the Vice Consul, but what tendered most of all to our dejection and unhappiness was the poor prospect, or rather no prospect, of our ever obtaining our precious liberty. We had never heard of, or from, any of our friends at home and the infernal government under whose clutches we were inthralled, together with the insulting, abusive and domineering conduct of the barbarians, we had few comfortable moments.

After two months detained in Mogodore, Irving could not conceal his despair beneath the thin veneer of optimism which he feigned to comfort his wife. In many ways his advice to Mary, although positive and encouraging, reflects his own low morale. He urged her 'despair not this is our day of trial' and reassured her that 'Providence will yet befriend us and restore me to you ...'. He was frantic to hear from his wife as 'ten long months have elapsed since the fatal shipwreck and not any letter from or account of you has reached me'. In particular he records how 'my heart breaks for your destitute situation'. He was at a loss to know what advice to give her about money for her support and recorded his hope that 'friends forsake you not in the day of tribulation' (Letter 29).

This was still his main concern in a letter written on 8th June 1790, his thirteenth month in captivity:

My dear Mary, it is a most melancholy truth that it is entirely out of my power to assist you in any respect. I can only pray for you, and trust to friends and a benevolent world for your support. O! the reflection is a cutting one, but the will of heaven be done. Had I the liberty of acting I doubt not but my endeavours are fully adequate to produce a tolerable support for us. That day through the help of Providence will yet come and all shall be well.

He apologises for the contents of a letter of 3rd June 1790 which he sent by a brig from 'Pulhely in Wales'. In this letter, which unfortunately does not survive, he 'gave a loose to the sense of our situation, and the little attention showed us either by our friends or by our Court' (Letter 31). This sense of neglect was clearly linked to the long periods of waiting without any positive news of their release.

As it was the Emperor of Morocco who had purchased the seamen from their various captors in the southern provinces, it was, as Hutchison pointed out in a letter of 11th January 1790, 'the Emperor to whom we are only (under God) to look for your ultimate delivrance from this country' (Letter 25). The prevarication that bedevilled the negotiations with the Emperor of Morocco is documented in the correspondence of James Matra, Consul General at Tangier. Matra clearly found it difficult to communicate directly with the Emperor and to circumvent this problem, his strategy involved trying to influence those who could gain his attention and confidence. This policy was appropriate given that the Emperor did not have a formal government of ministers but was assisted by a circle of trusted individuals.[53] In an outburst to Evan Nepean in December 1789, Matra described some of the difficulties of diplomacy:[54]

The men, are what I just now pay the most attention to but unhappily the distance the Court is from us and the distracted state it is in prevents our getting an answer under six or eight weeks, even when we can get a paper delivered to a friend or to the Emperor. In that respect though I have used a wonderful deal of precaution, I have been very unfortunate. I have sometimes sent to three different people, and by the time my courier gets to Court, they were sent to the other end of the Empire...

Matra's account is, of course, one-sided and in many ways represents a Eurocentric and simplistic view of Moroccan politics. Matra's letters will be used to continue Irving's narrative rather than to provide an interpretation of diplomatic affairs. As James Grey Jackson later pointed out Matra's inability to speak Arabic contributed to ineffective and unreliable negotiations at Court.[55] In the early nineteenth century Jackson referred to the 'tardiness and supineness of diplomacy' which contributed to the plight of seamen in captivity. He argued that the length of negotiations could have been shortened considerably if a fund of money had been deposited at Mogodore 'in the hands of a competent agent' who could actively negotiate for the release of seamen held captive in Morocco and the Sahara. If such arrangements had been put into effect Jackson questioned:

> How many an unfortunate Englishman would have been delivered from bondage? How many of our valuable countrymen would have returned to their families and connections? How many valuable sailors would be navigating on the ocean, who, dreadful to relate are now bereft of all hope of ever again seeing their native land, and are dragging out a miserable existence in the interior of the wild, uncouth African desert?

Jackson estimated that at least 40 English seamen shipwrecked between 1790 and 1806 were 'dispersed in various parts of the desert, after a lapse of time, in consequence of the Consul making no offers sufficiently advantageous to induce the Arabs to bring them to Mogodor'. He estimates that a further 80 seamen were 'redeemed after a tedious existence among the Arabs of from one to five years, or more, originating from various causes, such as a want of application being made through the proper channel, want of remitting money for their purchase, or want of a competent agent settled on the coast'.[56]

In Matra's view the Emperor would not sanction the release of Irving and his crew until two conditions were fulfilled; the receipt of a good present and a request for each of them by name from the British government.[57] A letter from Sultan Muhammad III to King George III, which survives amongst Matra's papers, links the release of the 'crew of the merchantman that was shipwrecked to the southward of our territories' to a request for 'several pieces of small cannon, mortars etc.'[58] Although dated 29th August 1789, Matra claimed in a letter of 19th December 1789 that he had only just received a copy. This was significant, as Mr. Layton, a merchant, who spoke to the Emperor on Matra's behalf reported that 'It will be difficult to do anything before answers come to the request some time past made for cannon and mortars'.[59] Matra enclosed with this letter to the Secretary of State's office a translation of one he had received from the Court of Morocco:[60]

> I have received your letter respecting the Christians whose vessel was wrecked. I will send them to nobody until a letter comes from your Court demanding in the name of the nation the said Christians, and in which they must name, each man by his name; then I will send them, but without that I never will send them to anyone – never. We have in time past redeemed and sent some away. They did not even write us a letter when they arrived and say in it, God reward you for this good action.

The release of the crew of the *Anna* depended upon a written request as Irving records in a letter of 31st January 1790 that 'the Emperor himself told me he could not grant til our Gracious Sovereign shall write to him requesting it'. Irving informed his wife 'this we daily expect as Mr. Matra, his Majesty's Consul General at Tangier, hath wrote a long time ago to the Secretary of State's office concerning us' (Letter 27). As early as December 1789 Matra had urged Evan Nepean to send a letter requesting the men. Matra tentatively asserted that the Emperor deserved a present as '... Irving's crew have cost him at least what he asserts and last year, you know, he bought the *Minerva's* crew, 5 or 6 men'.[61] By 14th February 1790, it appears that no progress had been made in this respect as Matra notes in his report to Whitehall that '... I shall not obtain the men, until his Majesty condescends to ask for them'.[62]

Although these were seemingly straightforward demands, the British government was apparently reluctant to acquiesce. The reason for this becomes clearer if Irving's case is considered in the context of the larger political agenda. Matra's correspondence during the previous eight months indicates that there was a considerable measure of disagreement between the Moroccan and British Governments regarding terms of trade and, in particular, the tariffs charged on various goods. The reluctance to send Muhammad III a present or to write a personal request for the men was linked to the animosity that had built up between the two governments. In his earlier letter to Evan Nepean, Matra recommended goodwill:[63]

> I should be very sorry if you took the least notice of that he [the Emperor] sent to England when he broke the Treaty, or of his raising the duties; it would be best policy to pass it over as beneath your notice, and leave me to work it out which I trust I shall do.

The breakthrough in negotiations which occurred in March 1790 was linked to the Emperor's offer to settle the long running dispute about tariffs. Jacob Atall, described by Matra as 'the Emperor's favourite Jew...', wrote the letter which informed the Consul-General of the terms of negotiation. In a letter to the Secretary of State's office dated the 22nd of the month, Matra reported that the Emperor had agreed to 'immediately grant us a free export of provision and restore the seamen' on condition that he was supplied with an English frigate.[64] James Irving II explained to his parents in a letter of 25th March 1790 that he soon expected to have his 'long lost liberty' as:

> ... the Emperor has wrote to the Governor of Gibraltar for the loan of a frigate to go to Alexandria with one of his sones who is going a pilgrimage to Mecca which if the Governor will grant, and there is no doubt but he will, the Emperor will deliver all of us up to him and likewise allow the trade of fresh provisions (duty free) from Tangier to Gibraltar which has been stopt for some time past (Letter 28).

Matra urged Admiral Peyton to meet the Emperor's request and send a frigate as 'it is the cheapest and most decent way to be relieved from a very irksome situation...'. The arrangement was particularly attractive as it 'does not so immediately interfere with the King's declaration refusing all grants to this court that are not directly applied for to His Majesty'.[65]

The Emperor informed Matra that once the frigate had reached Tetouan he would send Captain Irving and his men, together with some horses, as a present for the Prince of Wales during his planned visit to Gibraltar.[66] In a letter to Whitehall dated 17th April 1790 Matra confirmed that the Emperor '... had ordered a letter to be written to Captain Irving's men to be sent to His Royal Highness, Prince Edward'.[67] However, the death of Muhammad III a week after this order was given, entirely negated the arrangements for the men's release. The correspondence of the Prince of Wales during his visit to Gibraltar in April 1790 includes no reference to Irving and his men, and it is clear from their continued captivity in Mogodore that the agreement had collapsed.[68] In a letter written from Whitehall on 25th May 1790 Consul Matra was informed that 'His Majesty has great satisfaction in learning that orders have been given for the enlargement of the crew of the schooner, *Anna*'.[69] It is apparent that the official concerned had failed to recognise that the death of Sultan Muhammad III meant that the order given for the men's release was worthless.

The process of negotiation for the men's release had to recommence with Mawlay al-Yazid, the newly proclaimed Emperor.[70] With this change of political regime, Matra was optimistic that 'His Majesty's business in this country will now be favourably attended to...'.[71] In a number of private audiences with the new Emperor in late April and early May 1790, Matra received positive assurances 'in the politest manner' that the men would be released. Immediate success was not assured though as in subsequent correspondence with Whitehall, Matra records the Emperor's repeated failure to fulfil the promises made at these meetings.[72]

By the end of May 1790 Matra was clearly optimistic that the Emperor would approve the men's release as he arranged for Admiral Peyton to send a ship to Mogodore 'to receive on board Captain Irving and his crew'. In a letter to Whitehall dated 23rd June 1790, Matra explained that his efforts were again frustrated as '... the *Bull Dog* was sent here on the 30 ultimo, but on the 7th instant before I could have an answer from court and receive the necessary papers, she was recalled...'.[73] The fact that the crew's freedom had still not been secured is reflected in a letter which Irving wrote to his wife on 8th June 1790. He explained that 'the Emperor is expected at Morocco in 20 days when he will be again solicited by Mr. Hutchison Esquire, His Brittanick Majjestys Vice Consul here' (Letter 31). A month later no obvious progress had been made as

Irving wrote to his wife at the beginning of July 1790 and was unable to give '... any very flattering hopes of our being immediately released' (Letter 32).

The backdrop to the continuing negotiations for the crew's release was one of political instability and internal conflict between opposing factions, which added to the difficulties of maintaining effective diplomatic communication. The reign witnessed a violent reaction against many of the policies implemented by Sidi Muhammad. El Mansour, a historian, argues that 'the two year reign of Mawlay al-Yazid (1790-1792) was enough to undo the achievement of thirty years of stability and throw the country back into a dangerous state of civil war'.[74] Mawlay al-Yazid, described by Matra as a 'great bigot and decided enemy to every religion but his own...' sought to establish his authority in the months following his declaration as Emperor. Continuity in the administrative structures and procedures of the Moroccan state was considerably weakened by the Emperor's proclivity to dispose of the former officials and servants of his father. Jacob Atall who had played a significant part in the early negotiations for the crew's release, was executed just weeks after Mawlay al-Yazid was proclaimed Emperor. Matra described how 'he met with the most shocking barbarity; being cut in four and burnt was by far the mildest part of his treatment'.[75] El Mansour suggests that the reign of Mawlay al-Yazid 'became one of terror'; a reign that was particularly associated with a persecution of Jews.[76]

During the period from April until the end of July 1790 the crew of the *Anna* had considerably less freedom of movement than they had experienced in earlier months. It would still be accurate to describe the officers as 'prisoners on parole', a term used by one correspondent to characterise their situation (Letter 33), but the other crew members were not permitted 'to pass the threshold of the door...'. In the journal Irving describes how guards were posted to monitor their activities. Captain Irving and his officers took it in turns to purchase provisions from the market, although they were not permitted to go beyond the town gates. The restrictions on their movement were imposed as the crew had made an attempt to escape during the disturbed and confused period which followed the death of Muhammad III in April 1790. This opportunist endeavour, few details of which are provided in the journal, failed though as none of the ships in the harbour would agree to carry them.[77]

5. Freedom and return to England.

The removal of the sentries guarding their lodgings in Mogodore at the end of July 1790 finally signalled their freedom. Irving records in his journal how they were all summoned before the Governor of Mogodore and 'formally delivered up to the Vice Consul, as British subjects at his disposal'. The exact reasons which led Mawlay al-Yazid to free the crew of the *Anna* after 14 months in captivity are not clear, but the persistence of diplomatic endeavour undoubtedly played a part. Hutchison, the Vice Consul, who had played such a central role in negotiations for their release, arranged a celebration. As Captain Irving points out in his journal 'Our good Vice Consul bountifully enabled us to make merry, and the evening was spent in conviviality'.

After months of reassuring his wife that he would soon be with her, Captain Irving was at last able to say with some certainty that 'I and my crew have at last obtained our final discharge from this country...' In a letter dated 9th August 1790 from Mogodore he joyously reports the 'termination of my bondage, which I have weathered with ten thousand difficulties'. Quite a touching aspect of this letter is the way in which Irving listed his clothes on a folded down part of the manuscript, giving the impression of preparing for home. Included in the list are black satin breeches, black silk stockings, eight silk handkerchiefs as well as a number of the items that Hutchison had sent to Captain Irving on his arrival in Morocco (Marrakech). He informs his wife that they expect to leave Mogodore 'in a month or 5 weeks in the brig *Bacchus* Captain Prouting' (Letter 32). The journal records that on 24th September 1790 they finally sailed from Mogodore Bay 'with a cordial prayer that we might never again visit those barbarous regions in a similar predicament'.

The journal adds some detail to the account provided in his letter to Mary, as it indicates that the ten surviving crew members were distributed on board three different ships. Captain Irving, the surgeon, the chief mate and the second mate went on board the *Bacchus* as passengers, whilst two 'were shipped on board as seamen...'. The remaining four seamen were split between the sloop *Charlotte* in the command of Captain William Davis and the *Tryal* in the command of 'Captain Plumb Balding'. Reference to the shipping newspaper *Lloyd's List* indicates that all three ships had indeed been at Mogodore in the latter months of 1790. The edition for Friday 14th January 1791 records that the *Tryal* in the command of Captain Baldry arrived at Stangate Creek, London from Mogodore. On Friday 17th December the newspaper records that the *Charlotte* in the command of Captain Davis arrived at the Downs from Mogodore.

James Irving arrived in Dartmouth on board the brig *Bacchus* in the last week of October 1790 and wrote immediately to his wife to inform her of his safe arrival. His anxiety to hear from his wife was overwhelming and he urged her to 'dispatch a cupid post haste to relieve me' (Letter 34). Whilst a prisoner he longed for news of his wife, not least because their baby had been due in his absence. An associate who had tried to get letters forwarded to Captain Irving whilst in captivity explained on 22nd September 1790 that:

Since Mr. Irving has been at Mogodore, Mrs. Irving has heard from him often and has as often wrote, as well as many more of his friends here but he never has received any of the letters though they have been sent from the Secretary of State's office to the Consul at Mogodore (Letter 33).

During a period of quarantine at Stangate Creek, Irving wrote again to his wife on 6th November 1790 and urged her to 'write for God's sake'. Just as he was ready to despatch this brief letter to Mary he received one from her 'brought alongside by the quarantine boat...'.

He broke open his own letter to inform her that he had read her letter of 30th October 1790. His response to this letter, the first he had received since his shipwreck 18 months previously, was ecstatic:

I'm unable to express my most extreme joy and happiness, and my gratitude to our benificient Creator for his bounteous mercys in keeping and preserving you and our infant in your day of trial and under the distresses that oppressed you (Letter 35).

As references in Irving's letters indicate that the baby must have been born sometime between his departure for Africa on 3rd May 1789 and his return to Britain in November 1790, the registers of baptisms in Liverpool were checked within this narrow time frame. The Register of Births and Baptisms relating to the Congregation of Protestant Dissenters at Benns Garden Chapel, Liverpool contained the relevant entry.[1] James son of James Irving mariner and Mary his wife was born on 4th December 1789 and baptised on December 18th 1789. Jamie, as Captain Irving affectionately refers to him in later correspondence, was baptised in his father's absence, a usual practice in a seafaring community. The entry indicates that Mary Irving resided in Pownall Street, which broadly confirms the address of 7 Pownall Square which was used on all letters dated after 1789.[2]

Although released from captivity in Africa, there were still obstacles to negotiate before Irving could be reunited with his wife and his young son. The most serious danger that presented itself was that of the press gangs or 'land sharks' to use Hugh Crow's phrase.[3] Irving referred to the 'many fears of being carried on board some of His Majesty's ships' and he confided 'how to steer clear I'm very much at a loss to invent' (Letter 34). He subsequently solved this problem though with the assistance of his uncle, Mr. Smith, who '... hath procured protections for me and officers and shall send them down the moment he hears of my arrival' (Letter 35).

Irving was also concerned about a number of practical matters which needed to be resolved before he could return to Liverpool. These included his shabby appearance, the loss of his surgeon's certificate and his uncertainty about his employer's opinion of him. A letter written to Mary from his uncle's house on 12th November 1790 indicates that two of these problems were all but solved. He referred to the receipt of a letter and £20 from Mr. Dawson which he viewed as a 'good omen' for his future prospects. The £20 also gave Irving the power to assist his officers to return to Liverpool and meant that he could return 'in some degree of decency...'. He informed his wife that 'Mr. Smith and I are this minute going to a cloaths shop where I mean to get myself pretty well rigged and cast of the Arabic rags that as I thought ill-fitted me' (Letter 36). His surgeon's certificate had been lost at the time of the shipwreck, although he managed to recover a few fragments of it from the shoreline on the Barbary coast four days later. It is not clear whether he renewed his certificate during this time in London in November 1790 as the only reference to James Irving in the examinations book of the Company of Surgeons is that preceding his voyage on the <i>Anna</i> in April 1789. It is possible that a new certificate was issued in November 1790 without any requirement for re-examination. Irving was probably unaware that a medical board in Liverpool had secured the right to conduct such examinations,[4] but again, there is no reference to James Irving in the Liverpool board in 1790 or 1791.[5]

In the letter of 12th November 1790, written from 'our good friend Mr. Smith's fireside, where I moored myself late last night in tolerable health...', Irving informed his wife that he hoped to be with her in a few days time. He assured her that 'I long most ardently to be with you and our little lad' (Letter 36). There is no evidence to indicate the exact date of his arrival in Liverpool or of the emotions that he felt when he was reunited with his wife. The extent to which he recounted details of his experience is unclear, but in earlier letters he had promised Mary that he would relate the 'particulars of the misfortune ... to you at the fireside as soon as I get home...' (Letter 16). It is probable that he was in Liverpool for his son's first birthday on the 4th December 1790. Even if the particular day was not a focus for celebration as in modern practice, James Irving must have reflected on the difference in his circumstances that had occurred in the course of one year. It was on the day of his son's birth, that Captain Irving had been summoned to attend Mawlay 'Abd. al-Salam in his palace at Taroudant to give his advice on his occular complaint. James Irving may have found it difficult to adapt to his new found freedom and could have experienced the type of anxiety and stress disorders which have been noted following the release of modern day hostages.

Despite his prolonged absence from his wife and new baby, it seems that the financial pressures repeatedly referred to in his letters, necessitated an early return to sea. His happiness when he reached England in October 1790 was tempered by 'too acute a sense of our poor and dependent condition...' He expressed his hope that 'we shall soon lift our heads and enjoy a comfortable state of mediocrity, however embarrased we may be at present' (Letter 34). His agreement by mid-December 1790 to command another ship owned by John Dawson was undoubtedly linked to his need to 'retrieve what I've lost...' (Letter 16) and possibly a desire to re-establish his reputation with his employer.

The *Ellen* was re-registered in the name of John Dawson on 14th December 1790 and it is recorded that 'James Irving is at present master'. Reference is made to the 'former register granted at Liverpool number 107 dated the 13th April 1787 delivered up and cancelled'. Registered in the ownership of Thomas, William and James Moss, merchants of Liverpool, the *Ellen* weighed 134 tons with a length of 69'. The Certificate of Registry granted to John Dawson in December 1790 indicates that the *Ellen* weighed 152 tons and was 75' 10" long, and it would appear that the addition of a gallery to the ship between April 1787 and December 1790 accounts for the differences in length and weight.[6]

The condition of the *Ellen* built nine years earlier cannot be ascertained from the available evidence. The parliamentary list of slave ship clearances indicates that the ship had returned to Liverpool from a slaving venture on 26th November 1790. As this source records that the *Ellen* weighed 134 tons, the additions and improvements to the ship must have been undertaken between 26th November 1790 and 14th December 1790.[7] The increased weight of the ship meant that under the terms of the Dolben Act it could carry 253 slaves compared to the previous load of 223. Irving reassured his wife that she should 'not be anxious about the state of the vessel, as I have no doubt of doing well and making the voyage prosperously' (Letter 39).

As the *Ellen* sailed from the port of Liverpool on 2nd January 1791, Irving had spent just over one month with his family before returning to sea.[8] His cousin, the surgeon, sailed with him and it is difficult to know whether he had had sufficient time to visit his parents in Langholm in Scotland before undertaking another slaving voyage. When he wrote to his parents from Mogodore on 25th March 1790 he told them not to worry as 'I hope in a short time to be sitting at your fireside where I will tell you all that has happened to us since we came into Barbary' (Letter 28).

Other than his cousin, James Irving II, none of the former crew members of the *Anna* sailed with Irving on his second voyage as captain. Although Matthew Dawson, his second mate and nephew of John Dawson, and John Clegg, his first mate, returned to England with him on board the *Bacchus* they were not engaged for this voyage of the *Ellen*.[9] In a letter dated 25th January 1791, Captain Irving informed his wife that 'I'm very well supplied with officers, particularly the first and second mates, videlicet, Mr. Patton and Mr. Winter'. He asked his wife to visit Mr. Patton's wife once or twice as 'he deserves that attention as a good officer and scholar, although a cooper' (Letter 39). In this letter, written on 2nd February 1791, he describes how Mr. Bailey, his third mate, had proved a 'rascal' as:

> I watched him one night and caught him ready to get from alongside with his cloaths and two of the people. On presenting a pistol to his head, he ran and I secured him. He was shipped a stranger, although he belongs to Liverpool (Letter 39).

The letter does not mention the names of the two seamen who tried to escape, but Irving decided to 'tie them in spite of all their machinations'. The decision to retain them on board ship was undoubtedly a risk as Irving had an unpredictable and untrustworthy element amongst his crew of 26 men. As captain he must have had to balance this consideration against the likelihood of sailing to Africa without a full complement of men, something which could have caused difficulties in the purchase and control of slaves. He was already short of a carpenter for the voyage but intended to 'make a shift without one' (Letter 39).[10]

Although the ship left Liverpool on 2nd January 1791, it was delayed off the coast of Lancashire for at least a month. In a letter from 'Pile Fowdrey', dated 2nd February 1791 Irving pointed out that 'as I have been so long detained and retarded contrary to my inclination, you may be assured not one single tide shall be lost and the *Ellen* shall go to sea on the least prospect of getting round Holyhead' (Letter 39). The reason why the *Ellen* was in the Pile of Fouldrey, a channel located to the south-west of Ulverston in present day Cumbria, is not clear. It is possible that the *Ellen* had sailed to one of the small ports on this coastline to complete a cargo of goods with which to purchase slaves, or was returning from collecting cargo in the Isle of Man.[11]

Irving repeatedly reassured his wife of his strength, fortitude and health. Prior to sailing from 'Pile Fowdrey' he urged that she should not be fearful on his account as 'I am an old veteran in hard service and defy hardship. Had I been a coward, had been dead many years ago' (Letter 39). On his arrival in the Benin district on the west coast of Africa four months later he again stated 'I am healthy', a condition which he said he had enjoyed since he left Liverpool (Letter 40). When Irving wrote this letter on the 14th June 1791, he had already been sailing off the coast of Africa for more than two months as extracts taken from the ship's log and surgeon's journal by the Clerk to the Parliament indicate that the *Ellen* reached Anamabu in the Gold Coast region on 5th April 1791. During a five month period on the coast of Africa, Irving traded between Anamabu and the Benin district, a pattern described by the ship's surgeon in a letter to his parents written as the *Ellen* sailed from Liverpool on 2nd January 1791 (Letter

37). The *Ellen* left Anamabu on 16th September 1791 bound for Trinidad with the maximum legal number of 253 slaves on board, of whom only 206 survived the Middle Passage.[12]

By the time the ship reached Trinidad on 11th January 1792, Captain James Irving was dead. The muster roll records that he died on 24th December 1791, and was the sixth and final member of the crew to perish on this voyage of the *Ellen*. There is no evidence to indicate how he died. The chief mate, Thomas Patton, died approximately one month before the captain on 28th November 1791 and the second mate, Joseph Winters had been discharged in Africa on 25th May 1791. It was James Bailey, the third mate who had been held at gunpoint by James Irving, who took over command of the *Ellen* and returned with her to Liverpool in May 1792. Irving's cousin and namesake did not return with the *Ellen* to Liverpool as he was discharged in the West Indies on 14th February 1792.[13]

In the final surviving letter that James Irving had written to Mary from the Benin district in June 1791 he apologised for the brevity of the letter and promised that the next he wrote would be a very long one. He explained that '...when I sat down I meant to make this a long one, but the ship getting under weigh leaves me no time' (Letter 40). This promise to write is remarkably similar to the one that he made as he sailed from Liverpool on board the *Anna* on 3rd May 1789 before the fateful shipwreck (Letter 9). His death on board the *Ellen* might be linked directly to his experiences in slavery as it is likely that he had not fully recovered from the debilitating effects of the long period spent in Morocco.

6. Conclusion.

James Irving's career in Liverpool in the late eighteenth century developed against the backdrop of debate on the morality and sustainability of the slave trade.[1] Although Irving stated in a letter of December 1786 that he was 'nearly wearied of this unnatural accursed trade' and was considering 'adopting some other mode of life ...', this still does not give a clear indication of how he viewed the slaves or the institution of slavery (Letter 4). At first sight, his comment might be interpreted as a rejection or condemnation of the trade in slaves. The context of the statement, however, indicates that he was more concerned with his own conditions of work and the remuneration of his 'station' than with the plight of the slaves. Lempriere's summary of Irving's career lends support to this view as he records that Irving found his position as surgeon 'a disadvantageous employment' and that he 'subsequently obtained command of a small vessel in the same trade...'.[2] If Irving had any moral qualms, they were not sufficiently strong to prevent his continued involvement in the trade.[3]

Perhaps more revealing is a comment, contained in the same letter from Tobago, in which he informs his wife that 'I think I'll desist [writing] as our black cattle are intolerably noisy and I'm almost melted in the midst of five or six hundred of them'. This comment records his own discomfort, but, otherwise, Irving makes no mention in any of his letters of the conditions experienced by the slaves during the voyage to the West Indies. The phrase, 'black cattle', which Irving used to describe the African slaves is striking.[4] The term may already have been in Irving's vocabulary as the market town of Dumfries, set in a pastoral farming district close to his home town of Langholm in Scotland, was noted for the sale of 'an immense number of black cattle...'[5] Irving's use of this phrase to describe the human cargo powerfully conveys the way in which individual Africans were dehumanised and treated as objects or commodities for exchange. Earlier in the letter Irving informs his wife that 'we ... have not yet disposed of any of our very disagreeable cargo, but expect it on the 7th instant when our sale opens' (Letter 4).

To the modern day reader, drawn from a society in which 'disapproval of the slave trade' is the 'kind of cultural assumption which requires no evidential support...', Irving presents something of a paradox.[6] His letters reveal a man avowedly Christian in outlook, yet involved in a trade which has been variously described as 'iniquitous', 'morally repugnant' and a 'human atrocity that has yet to be duplicated'.[7] There is insufficient evidence on which to provide a detailed exposition of his views and beliefs, but it is clear that he was able to reconcile his occupation with his Christian beliefs. There is no suggestion in his correspondence with his wife, typically frank and reflective, that he was wrestling with a moral dilemma.

Contemporary justifications for the slave trade were diverse in nature and often embraced notions of divine will. Captain Hugh Crow, for example, stated his 'decided opinion' that the 'traffic in Negroes is permitted by the Providence that rules over all, as a necessary evil...'[8] In his letters Irving often exhorted his wife to trust in Providence who 'sees farther than we can and orders all aright', a philosophy which could easily extend to encompass the type of moral certainties expressed by Crow (Letter 16). Crow also maintained that the treatment of slaves in the colonies was more humane than that which would be meted out by their own countrymen, views shared by Robert Norris and Archibald Dalzel, Liverpool delegates who opposed restrictions on the trade in the parliamentary session of 1788.[9] James Irving, and other participants in the trade, may well have developed personal variations on these justifications which could embrace their own philosophy of life.

Hugh Crow's argument that 'masters in the African trade were not such wretches as commonly represented' is not particularly helpful. His opinion that 'men of integrity and humanity were found on board of Guineamen as well as in other lines of life' has a flawed logic which could be extended to justify many apparent outrages against humanity.[10] Assessing levels of 'goodness', 'humanity' and 'integrity' is an extremely subjective exercise, particularly as individuals exhibit different modes of behaviour in different circumstances. It would be meaningless to try and place James Irving on a point of a scale embracing good and evil, humanity and inhumanity. Perhaps more important is a recognition of the complexity of individual attitudes towards slavery and the interaction with broader societal values and cultural assumptions.[11]

The use of the term 'slavery' to describe Irving's condition in Morocco as well as the economic and social status of the 3,000 or so Africans that he helped to transport to the colonies of the West Indies and America is misleading if it implies homogeneity of experience. At a superficial level there are many apparent similarities, yet the differences in their circumstances were fundamental. Irving's experience, for example, was probably shared by only several hundred seamen of various nationalities. Moreover, his enslavement resulted from chance circumstances, not from the sophisticated economic system of the Atlantic slave trade.

A key factor which distinguished Irving's enslavement from that of African slaves in the Americas was that government representatives were willing to spend time and money to secure his release. It is true that negotiations were drawn out and complex and that his release was not a foregone conclusion. However, Irving's legal right to freedom was never in question amongst the consular representatives and they were prepared to use a range of devices to secure his liberty. For most of his period in captivity, Irving was regularly informed of the progress of negotiations and, therefore, had an indication of his likely fate. More basic still, Irving had a clear sense of his geographical location. In contrast, many of the Africans sold as slaves had little or no idea of what was intended for them. For example, it was widely 'rumoured that the whites were cannibals, carrying off their captives in order to eat them'.[12] The disorientation was so great that some, unfamiliar with the oceans, attempted to swim ashore during the voyage across the Atlantic.[13]

Irving felt distraught about his prolonged separation from his wife and family in Britain and his cousin, James Irving II, in the possession of Mawlay 'Abd. al-Rahman. He feared for their safety and mourned for his own emotional loss. The psychological deprivation experienced during his captivity contributed to physical debilitation, and it is clear from his journal that he experienced several recurrences of fever in a strange disease environment. Irving records the verbal and physical abuse to which he and his crew were subjected, and the fact that 'the people in every place would never again have used a dish that we had eat or drank out of, so great was their detestation and contempt of us'. Their Christian faith, which Irving found so 'soothing ... in affliction', was a factor which excited the hatred of their captors.[14]

In a letter to his wife dated 9th August 1790, Irving refers to the 'termination of my bondage, which I have weathered with ten thousand difficultys' (Letter 32). He clearly felt that he had been ill-treated. This can be overstated. After all, ten of the eleven crew members of the *Anna* survived and returned to England, whilst James Drachen, a Portuguese black, died of a fever in 'Telling' in October 1789.

Liberty was precious to Irving and, on a number of occasions, he recorded his sentiment that 'I could have died rather than devote my life to be spent in so abject a state, bereft of all Christian society, a slave to a savage race who despised and hated me for my belief'.[15] Irving saw his enslavement as a slight of the hand of fate; that through misfortune he had been temporarily deprived of his natural liberty. He seems to have regarded liberty as a quality or condition that was particularly appropriate to Englishmen. In his journal, for example, he records that 'Had I been master of the Indies, I would most cheerfully have parted with them for liberty, a priviledge so dear to Englishmen'.

There is the possibility that the period spent with the 'savages', as Irving referred to his captors, reinforced his notions of European superiority. His early return to sea was undoubtedly linked to the exigencies of his financial situation, but as he died during the voyage of the *Ellen*, there are few letters from which to gauge whether his experience of enslavement in North Africa had significantly changed his attitudes to the trade in which he was engaged. There is no evidence to indicate that he was able or willing to empathise with the African slaves.

Irving's story is highly individual, yet his death at sea reflects a commonplace experience amongst captains in the slave trade as many died during their first or second voyage in command.[16] The career of his younger cousin and namesake, James Irving II, was also shortlived. A gravestone in the churchyard at Langholm reads:

In memory of Janetus Irving, Baker, who died 8th April 1815, aged 74. Helen Little his spouse who died 17th August 1797 aged 60. Also James and Ann children who died 17th June 1771 in infancy. And James their son, surgeon, who died at Lagus in Africa 22nd June 1793, aged 21.

Captain James Irving has no memorial stone in Langholm old churchyard. He had been baptised at the church, now in ruins, the day after he was born on 16th December 1759. He was the son of John Irving, a smith in Langholm and Isobel

Little his wife. The same couple baptised a daughter, Ann, on 26th December 1762, but the infant died the next day and was buried 'in Langholm in the churchyard' on 28th December 1762. Five years later on 19th December 1767, John and Isobel Irving buried their son, William Irving, who was aged just three and a half months.[17]

The inscription in Langholm old churchyard was dedicated to:

John Irving, Innkeeper in Langholm, who died 21st October 1807, aged 76. Isobel Little, his wife who died 4th November 1791 aged 66. And children Ann and William who died in infancy.

That Captain James Irving was the only surviving son of John and Isobel Little is confirmed by the legal proceedings which followed the death of John Irving, innkeeper. On November 30th 1807, James Irving the son of Captain James Irving (hereafter James Irving III) began proceedings in the Dumfries Service of Heirs to establish that he was the nearest lawful heir to the deceased John Irving, his grandfather. A petition addressed to the 'honourable the magistrates of the Burgh of Dumfries' on 16th February 1808 claims that James Irving of Liverpool is the 'only lawful son of the deceased James Irving late surgeon in the Affrican trade who was the son of the deceased John Irving innkeeper in Langholm...'. In Liverpool in February 1808 witnesses were called before the magistrate, Thomas Golightly, to establish the legality of James Irving III's claim.[18] John Bell, Gentleman of Liverpool, aged 50, swore that he was '... well acquainted with the now deceased James Irving surgeon in the Affrican trade and that he also knowes and is well acquainted with his son James ... who was the only lawful child of the said deceased James Irving...'. John Redcliff described as a landing waiter in the customs of Liverpool concurred 'with the preceding witness John Bell in omnibus and which is truth as he shall answer to God'.[19]

The death of Captain James Irving on Christmas Eve 1791, at the age of 32, left the two year old child Jamie without a father.[20] It is not clear whether his mother, Mary Irving née Tunstall, remarried. Jamie (James Irving III) was probably brought up by his mother and maternal grandmother, Mrs. Tunstall, who lived with Mary during the period of Captain Irving's shipwreck and slavery. Mrs. Tunstall died in 1809 when James Irving III, her grandson, was aged 19.[21] The subsequent history of this family lies outside the scope of this text, but the fact that Captain Irving's descendants saw fit to preserve the documentary record of his extraordinary experiences has allowed this story to be told.

NOTES:

1. Sources.
1. L.R.O., DDX 1126/1-45.
2. P.R.O., FO 52/8, FO 52/9.
3. L.C.R.O., 387 MD 28. See Letter 30.
4. The letters are described in an unpublished article by A.E. Truckell, *Some 18th century transatlantic trade documents*, a copy of which is deposited in the D.A.C. Transcripts of the letters are held at D.A.C., although the originals are still in private ownership.
5. This was noted in parentheses by the person who transcribed Irving's journal. L.R.O., DDX 1126/1.

2. Early Career in the Liverpool Slave Trade.
1. In a letter of 2nd December 1786 from Tobago, Irving asks his wife Mary to 'write to Langholm and satisfy the longings of good indulgent parents'. L.R.O., DDX 1126/6. Identifying his date of birth and family background involved linkage of a number of sources. See below pp. 70-71.
2. The total number of slaves exported from Africa has been the subject of on-going academic debate since the publication of Philip D. Curtin's *The Atlantic slave trade: a census* in 1969. Revised estimates of the numbers exported from Africa over four centuries, the coastal distribution of the trade and the numbers carried by ships of different nations have been proposed by a number of scholars. Paul Lovejoy argues that 'when the revisions are examined carefully ... it is apparent that Curtin's initial tabulation was remarkably accurate'. Paul E. Lovejoy, 'The volume of the Atlantic slave trade: a synthesis', *J.A.H.*, vol. 23 (1982), pp. 473-501.
3. David Richardson estimates that British, French, Portuguese, Dutch, American and Danish ships exported 6,686,000 slaves from the west coast of Africa in the period 1700-1809. The decadal figures suggest that between 1780-1799, 1,558,000 slaves were exported, of which 766,000 were carried in British ships, 291,000 in French and 408,000 in Portuguese ships. D. Richardson, 'Slave exports from West and West Central Africa, 1700-1810: new estimate of volume and distribution', *J.A.H.*, vol. 30 (1989), pp. 2, 3, 9-11.
4. D. Richardson ed., *Bristol, Africa and the eighteenth century slave trade to America, vol. 1. The years of expansion 1698-1729*, Bristol Record Society Publications, vol. xxxviii (1986), p. vii.
5. D.P. Lamb, 'Volume and tonnage of the Liverpool slave trade, 1772-1807', in Roger Anstey and P.E.H. Hair ed., *Liverpool, the African slave trade and abolition*, Historic Society of Lancashire and Cheshire, Occasional series, vol. 2, enlarged edition (1989), pp. 91-3; Richardson argues that Liverpool's rapid expansion should not obscure the significance of the slave trade in Bristol which was more extensive than that of Liverpool in the first half of the eighteenth century. Richardson, *Bristol*, vol. i, p. viii.
6. Stephen D. Behrendt, 'The captains in the British slave trade from 1785 to 1807', *T.H.S.L.C.*, vol. 140 (1991), table 4, p. 95.
7. *Ibid.*, p. 82.

8. Langholm parish registers, 1668-1854, D.A.C., MF 67; Certificate of British Registry, M.M.M.A., C/EX/L/4, vol. 7, no. 20.

9. Behrendt, 'Captains', pp. 89-91.

10. *Ibid.,* table 5, p. 98, 97-100.

11. *Ibid.,* pp. 91-94.

12. Hugh Crow, *Memoirs of the late Captain Hugh Crow of Liverpool* (London, 1970), pp. 1-66.

13. His father, John Irving, is described as a smith in the baptism registers between 1759 and 1762 and in the entry which records the burial of his wife Isobel in 1791. He is also described as an innkeeper on his gravestone in Langholm old parish churchyard. Langholm parish registers, 1664-1854, D.A.C., MF 67; *Memorials of Langholm Parish,* reference 18.

14. David Irving, *The History of Scottish Poetry* (Edinburgh, 1861), pp. xi-xii .

15. I am grateful for this information supplied in correspondence by Miss Glen Jones, Librarian, the Royal College of Surgeons of England. As there is no record of James Irving in the archives of the the Royal College of Surgeons of Edinburgh, it is possible that he was apprenticed closer to home in the nearby town of Dumfries, or even in Langholm. His apprenticeship is not listed in P.J. and R.V. Wallis, *Eighteenth century medics,* 2nd edition (Newcastle-upon-Tyne, 1988). It is unlikely that the record of apprenticeship of 'James Irvine' to Nathaniel Spens and Robertson, surgeons of Edinburgh, on 1st September 1768 relates to the future slave ship captain. The different surname spelling may be of little significance, but his apprenticeship to this occupation at the age of eight would have been atypically young. R.B. Sheridan refers to the careers of three surgeons in the West Indies who were apprenticed between the ages of 15 and 17. R.B. Sheridan, 'Mortality and the medical treatment of slaves in the British West Indies', in Stanley L. Engerman and Eugene D. Genovese ed., *Race and slavery in the Western Hemisphere: quantitative studies* (Princeton, 1975), pp. 293-302.

16. William Lempriere, *A tour from Gibraltar to Tangier, Sallee, Mogodore, Santa Cruz, Tarudant, and thence over Mount Atlas to Morocco,* 3rd ed. (London, 1804), pp. 275-6.

17. Muster rolls were completed after the ship had returned to Britain. P.R.O., BT 98/42-50.

18. P.R.O., BT 98/44, 2nd June 1784.

19. P.R.O., BT 98/43, 11th July 1783.

20. *Lloyd's List* of 4th February 1783 records that the *Vulture* in the command of Captain Wilson had arrived at Tortola.

21. I am grateful to P.E.H. Hair for drawing this to my attention. B.K. Drake emphasises a related point that the 'typical Liverpool slave trader was a "general merchant" ...' B.K. Drake, 'The Liverpool–African voyage, c.1790-1807: commercial problems', in Anstey and Hair, *Liverpool, the African slave trade and abolition',* p. 127.

22. P.R.O., BT 98/42, 17th October 1782.

23. Behrendt, 'Captains', table B, p. 126; P.R.O., BT 98/45, 16th July 1785.

24. P.R.O., BT 98/47, 27th March 1787.

25. It is unclear when and where they married.

26. P.R.O., BT 98/48, 19th January 1788.

27. *Liverpool shipbuilders and the ships they built*, Liverpool Nautical Research Society, unpublished reference work kept at M.M.M.A.

28. Certificate of British Registry, M.M.M.A., C/EX/L/4, vol. 4, no. 96.

29. M.K. Stammers, ' "Guineamen": some technical aspects of slave ships', in Anthony Tibbles, ed., *Transatlantic slavery: against human dignity*, (London, 1994), p. 40.

30. P.R.O., BT 98/49, 2nd March 1789.

31. L.R.O., DDX 1126/9.

32. L.R.O., DDX 1126/34. In the catalogue this letter has a suggested date of spring 1791. However, the address of 45 Paradise Street corresponds with an earlier phase in Irving's career. A letter of 20th October 1787 is also addressed to Mary Irving at 45 Paradise Street, although by May 1789 Irving addressed his letters to 7 Pownall Square, Liverpool.

33. A transcript is held at the D.A.C.

34. The importance of such contracts is noted by F.E. Sanderson, 'The Liverpool delegates and Sir William Dolben's Bill', *T.H.S.L.C.*, vol. 124 (1972), p. 75; J.E. Inikori, 'Measuring the Atlantic slave trade: an assessment of Curtin and Anstey', *J.A.H.*, vol. xvii, no. 2 (1976), pp. 208-9.

35. H.L.R.O., Lords Journal 3rd July and 10th July 1788; H.L. Main Papers, 3rd July 1788 and 10th July 1788.

36. *Ibid.*, 10th July 1788.

37. Under the terms of the Dolben Act ships could carry five slaves for every three tons of 'burthen' (1.67 per ton) up to a maximum of 201 tons and one slave for each remaining ton. From 1st August 1788, the *Princess Royal*, a ship of 596 tons was entitled to carry 730/731 slaves, a reduction of 70 from the 800 slaves which the ship had carried to Havana earlier that year. 'An act to regulate, for a limited time, the shipping and carrying of slaves in British vessels from the coast of Africa', clause I, Elizabeth Donnan ed., *Documents illustrative of the history of the slave trade to America, vol II* (Washington, 1931), p. 583.

38. L.C.R.O., 387 MD 28. This comment on Captain Sherwood is noted on the reverse side of the letter, although the author is unknown. See Letter 30.

39. Crow, *Memoirs,* p. 32.

40. 'An Act to regulate, for a limited time, the shipping and carrying of slaves in British vessels from the coast of Africa', Donnan, *History of the slave trade*, pp. 582-589.

41. Behrendt, 'Captains', pp. 99-100.

42. See letters 31 and 39.

43. Alexander Falconbridge, a former surgeon in the slave trade, referred to the 'expected premium usually allowed to the captains, of 6 per cent sterling on the produce of the negroes...'. Alexander Falconbridge, *An account of the slave trade on the coast of Africa* (London, 1788), p.27.

44. Behrendt, 'Captains', pp. 112-114.

45. Valuable information about sources is contained in M.M. Schofield, 'The slave trade from Lancashire and Cheshire ports outside Liverpool, c. 1750-1790', *T.H.S.L.C.*, vol. 126 (1977), pp. 30-72.

3. Characteristics of the slave trade.

1. Minchinton argues that the trade was triangular in outline as ships typically carried cargo on three stages of the voyage. George Shepperson questions whether the term 'triangular' adequately conveys the complexities of the trade as there were repercussions felt along other trade routes. Walter E. Minchinton, 'The triangular trade revisited' in H.A. Gemery and Jan S. Hogendorn, ed., *The Uncommon Market: essays in the economic history of the Atlantic slave trade* (New York, 1979), pp. 331-351; George Shepperson, 'Comment', in Engerman and Genovese, *Race and slavery*, p. 102.

2. Minchinton suggests that few ships returned to England without a cargo. Minchinton, 'Triangular trade', pp. 339, 351; Roger Anstey, 'The volume and profitability of the British slave trade, 1761-1807', in Engerman and Genovese, *Race and slavery*, p. 17; David Richardson ed., *Bristol, Africa and the eighteenth century slave trade to America, vol. 3. The years of decline 1746-69*, Bristol Record Society Publications, vol. xlii (1991), p. xxiv.

3. Drake, 'Liverpool-African voyage', in Anstey and Hair, *Liverpool, the African slave trade and abolition*, pp. 132-5; Richardson suggests that the journey took ten months between 1783 and 1787, David Richardson, 'The costs of survival: the transport of slaves in the Middle Passage and the profitability of the 18th-century British slave trade', *E.E.H.*, vol. 24 (1987), p. 192.

4. L.R.O., DDX 1126/4, DDX 1126/5 (see Letters 2 & 3).

5. Johannes Postma points to the high death rates amongst slaves awaiting embarkation on European ships. Johannes Postma, 'Mortality in the Dutch slave trade, 1675-1795', in Gemery and Hogendorn, *The Uncommon Market*, pp. 240-242.

6. For a discussion of sources of supply and delivery mechanisms see Mahdi Adamu, 'The delivery of slaves from the central Sudan to the Bight of Benin in the eighteenth and nineteenth centuries' and Paul E. Lovejoy and Jan S. Hogendorn, 'Slave marketing in West Africa', in Gemery and Hogendorn, *The Uncommon Market*, chapters 6 and 8.

7. P.E.H. Hair, *The Atlantic slave trade and Black Africa* (Historical Association, 1978), pp. 13-17; Marion Johnson, 'The Atlantic slave trade and the economy of West Africa', in Anstey and Hair, *Liverpool, the African slave trade and abolition*, pp. 14-17; David Richardson, 'West African consumption patterns and their influence on the eighteenth century English slave trade', in Gemery and Hogendorn, *The Uncommon Market*, pp. 303-30.

8. Richardson, 'Consumption patterns', p. 319.

9. Hair, *Atlantic slave trade and Black Africa*, p. 21.

10. Drake, 'Liverpool-African voyage', pp. 148-150.

11. *Ibid.*, table 1, p. 146.

12. Falconbridge described how 'after the kings have been on board and have received the usual presents, permission is granted by them for trafficking with any of the black traders'. He noted that 'after permission has been obtained for breaking trade, as it is termed, the captains go ashore, from time to time, to examine the negroes that are exposed to sale, and to make their purchases'. Falconbridge, *Slave trade*, pp. 7, 8, 12.

13. I am grateful to P.E.H. Hair for drawing my attention to this information. P.E.H. Hair, 'Antera Duke of Old Calabar – A little more about an African entrepreneur', *H.A.*, vol. 17

(1990), pp. 359-365.

14. Richardson, 'Slave exports', table 5, p. 13, 11-20; Engerman considers that the shifts in trading patterns highlight the flexibility of response amongst both African and European traders, Engerman and Genovese, *Race and slavery*, p. 496.

15. H.L.R.O., HL Main Papers 28th July 1800. This tabular statement includes *i.* ship's name *ii.* tonnage *iii.* date of clearing from Great Britain and from what port *iv.* date of arrival on coast of Africa and what part thereof *v.* Total number of slaves taken on board from the time of the ship's arrival on the coast until the final departure *vi.* number that died from the ship's arrival on the coast until her final departure *vii.* number relanded from the ship's arrival on the coast until her final departure *vii.* Number transhipped from the time of the ship's arrival on the coast until her final departure *ix.* date of final departure and from what part of the coast *x.* number of slaves on board at the time of the ship's departure from the coast *xi.* number of slaves that died on the Middle Passage *xii.* date of arrival in the West Indies and at what port *xiii.* number of slaves landed and sold *xiv.* date of ship's clearance from the West Indies or America (sections *v-viii, x, xi & xiii* distinguish between males and females and 'grown slaves' and children). This source is described more fully in Lamb, 'Liverpool slave trade', pp. 107-8.

16. In addition to the 'Return ... of ships employed in the slave trade in each year from 1791 to 1797', there is a separate and more detailed statement of slave purchases for the *'Ellen* of Liverpool, 1791'. This records the number of slaves by sex and age purchased between 11th April 1791 and 14th September 1791. This table records the number who were transhipped on the African coast, the number who died in the Middle Passage and the number landed and sold in the West Indies. H.L.R.O., HL Main Papers 28th June, 1799.

17. A transcript of this letter is held at Dumfries Archive Centre.

18. Philip D. Curtin, *The Atlantic slave trade: a census* (Madison, 1969), p. 282; K.G. Davies points to even higher death rates in the 17th and early 18th century. K.G. Davies, 'The living and the dead: white mortality in West Africa, 1684-1732', in Engerman and Genovese, *Race and slavery*, p. 97.

19. Crow, *Memoirs,* pp. 29-34.

20. In 1788 Falconbridge described how 'they ... minutely inspect their persons, and inquire into the state of their health; if they are afflicted with any infirmity...they are rejected'. Falconbridge, *Slave trade,* pp. 16-17; W. N. Boog Watson discusses the role and duties of the slave ship surgeon in W.N. Boog Watson, 'The Guinea trade and some of its surgeons', *Journal of the Royal College of Surgeons of Edinburgh,* vol. xiv, no. 4 (July 1969), pp. 206-7.

21. Richardson, 'Costs of survival', pp. 178-196.

22. Falconbridge suggests that the surgeon could have little impact on levels of slave mortality. Falconbridge, *Slave trade,* pp. 28-9.

23. The *Ellen* had 149 males on board when she sailed from the African coast of whom 31 died (21%), compared with 16 of the 104 female slaves (15%). In the Dutch trade Postma points out that proportionately more men than women died in the Middle Passage, although 'the reasons for this remain speculative'. Postma, 'Mortality', p. 260; Herbert S. Klein and Stanley L. Engerman, 'Slave mortality of British ships, 1791-1797', in Anstey and Hair, *Liverpool, the African slave trade and abolition*, pp. 117-118.

24. Clause XIV of the Act stated that £100 should be paid to the master and £50 to the surgeon if 'there shall not have died more than in the proportion of two slaves in the hundred, from the time of the arrival of such ship or vessel on the coast of Africa, to the time of her arrival at her port of discharge in any of the islands in the West Indies...'. A bounty of £50 for the master and £25 for the surgeon was payable if 'there shall not have died more than in the proportion of three slaves in the hundred...'. 'An Act to regulate, for a limited time, the shipping and carrying of slaves in British vessels from the coast of Africa', Donnan, *History of the slave trade*, p. 587.

25. Bernard Martin and Mark Spurrell ed., *The journal of a slave trader (John Newton) 1750-1754* (London, 1962), p. 47.

26. Kenneth F. Kiple and Brian T. Higgins, 'Mortality caused by dehydration during the Middle Passage', in Joseph E. Inikori and Stanley L. Engerman, *The Atlantic slave trade: effects on economies, societies and peoples in Africa, the Americas and Europe* (London, 1992), p. 326.

27. A Genuine "Dicky Sam", *Liverpool and slavery: an historical account of the Liverpool-African slave trade* (Liverpool 1884, reprint 1985), pp. 29-32.

28. Certificate of British Registry, M.M.M.A., C/EX/L/4, vol. 8, no. 133.

29. Lamb, 'Liverpool slave trade', table 10, p. 101.

30. Lamb points out that the legislation was 'largely obeyed'. *Ibid.*, p.104.

31. Herbert S. Klein and Stanley L. Engerman, 'A note on mortality in the French slave trade in the eighteenth century', in Gemery and Hogendorn, *The Uncommon Market*, pp. 264-5; As Johannes Postma points out '... the more or less crowded conditions added little to generally unhygienic conditions on board ship', Postma, 'Mortality', p. 260.

32. Sanderson relates area of origin to mortality levels in Sanderson, 'Liverpool delegates', p. 76; Postma suggests that in the Dutch trade the length of the Middle Passage 'provides the most systematic explanation'. Postma, 'Mortality', p. 250.

33. Klein and Engerman, 'Note on mortality', pp. 267-272.

34. Falconbridge, *Slave trade*, pp. iii, 11, 37.

35. Sanderson, 'Liverpool delegates', p. 69, note 34, p.81; In the French trade between 1714-1778 15-20% of crew members did not return to France, Robert Stein, 'Mortality in the eighteenth century French slave trade', *J.A.H.*, vol. 21 (1980), p. 36.

36. P.R.O., BT 98/47, 27th March 1787.

37. Curtin, *Atlantic slave trade*, p. 283.

38. P.R.O., BT 98/48, 19th January 1788.

39. P.R.O., BT 98/52, 31st July 1792.

40. Curtin, *Atlantic slave trade*, pp. 282-3, 286.

41. Crow, *Memoirs*, p. 42.

42. Stein, 'Mortality', p. 39.

43. None of the voyages in which Irving participated are amongst the list of 93 surviving accounts, Richardson, 'Consumption patterns', table 12.2, pp. 312-315.

44. David Richardson, 'Liverpool and the English slave trade', in Tibbles, *Transatlantic slavery*, pp. 75-6.

45. David Richardson, 'Profits in the Liverpool slave trade: accounts of William

Davenport, 1757-1784', in Anstey and Hair, *Liverpool, the African slave trade and abolition*, pp. 65, 69, 73, 76-7; Richardson, 'Costs of survival', pp. 178-196.

46. A Genuine "Dicky Sam", *Liverpool and slavery*, p. 109.

47. Certificate of British Registry, M.M.M.A., C/EX/L/4, vol. 7, no. 20.

48. Richardson points to the high costs involved in preparing a ship for Africa, Richardson, 'Costs of survival', pp. 184-6.

49. H.L.R.O., Lords Journal 3rd July & 10th July 1788; H.L. Main papers, 3rd July 1788 & 10th July 1788.

50. P.R.O., ADM 7/109, Pass number 7469, ADM 7/108.

4. Shipwreck and Slavery.

1. M.M.M.A., OA 1866, Atlas of Charts, 1794.

2. L.R.O., DDX 1126/16.

3. It is not clear whether he compiled some of the notes for his journal contemporaneously. The style in which the journal is written indicates that he was summarising events which had already occurred, rather than writing a daily diary of his experiences. It may, for example, have been written on the return voyage from Morocco. In the absence of the original journal, it is difficult to reach any firm conclusions. L.R.O., DDX 1126/1.

4. Martin and Spurrell, *Journal of a slave trader*, pp. 8-9.

5. James Grey Jackson, *An account of the Empire of Morocco*, 3rd edition (London, 1968), p.271.

6. Lempriere, *Tour*, p. 276.

7. 'An account of all vessels which have cleared for London, Bristol and Liverpool to Africa since the year 1788', P.R.O., T64/286.

8. N.R. Bennett, 'Christian and Negro slaves in eighteenth century North Africa', *J.A.H.*, vol. i (1960), pp. 65-82.

9. Jackson, *Morocco*, pp. 279-281.

10. P.R.O., FO 52/9, 115-116.

11. L.R.O., DDX 1126/16.

12. P.R.O., FO 52/8, 177-180.

13. L.R.O., DDX 1126/16.

14. Mohamed El Mansour, *Morocco in the reign of Mawlay Sulayman* (Wisbech, 1990), p. 5; Jackson, *Morocco*, p. ix.

15. Sidi Muhammad b. 'Abd. Allah of the 'Alawid dynasty, Emperor of Morocco between 1757-1790, is usually credited with restoring peace and stability to the country and expanding trade with Europe. His exiled son Mawlay 'Abd. al-Rahman established political control in the southern territories. Following the death of the Emperor in 1792 Mawlay 'Abd. al-Rahman established 'an independent principality in the Sous', an area surrounding Agadir and Taroudant. El Mansour comments that he had no pretensions to the throne, unlike a number of his brothers. Richard Gray ed. *The Cambridge History of Africa*, vol. 4 (Cambridge, 1975), pp. 148, 150; El Mansour, *Morocco*, pp. 89, 96.

16. D.J. Schroeter, 'Merchants and pedlars of Essaouira: a social history of a Moroccan trading town, 1844-1886', (unpub. Ph.D. thesis, University of Manchester, 1984), p. 47.

17. El Mansour, *Morocco*, pp. 5-6, 35-8.

18. Jackson, *Morocco*, p. 56.

19. P.R.O., FO 52/8, 108-109.

20. L.R.O., DDX 1126/1.

21. Schofield, 'Slave trade from Lancashire and Cheshire ports', p. 31.

22. P.R.O., ADM 7/109, ADM 7/108.

23. James Grey Jackson comments on the southern territories 'being thus only nominally in his [the Emperor] dominions', Jackson, *Morocco*, p. 276; El Mansour, *Morocco*, p. 16, 22-26.

24. El Mansour, *Morocco*, p. 24.

25. *Ibid.*, pp. 14-16.

26. P.R.O., FO 52/8, 108-109.

27. P.R.O., FO 52/9, 113-114.

28. P.R.O., FO 52/8, 131.

29. P.R.O., FO 52/8, 144.

30. Lempriere, *Tour,* pp. 2-3.

31. *Ibid.*, pp. 5-13, 122-133. Hutchison informed Captain Irving that he had received a letter from his cousin written at Taroudant dated 27th October 1789 (Letter 23), a date more or less corresponding with Lempriere's arrival.

32. P.R.O., FO 52/8, 177-180.

33. *Ibid.*

34. *Ibid.*, 184.

35. Lempriere, *Tour*, pp. 128, 133-6, 169.

36. *Ibid.*, pp. 139, 171-2.

37. *Ibid.*, pp. 138-9.

38. L.R.O., DDX 1126/1.

39. Jackson, *Morocco*, p. 73.

40. Lempriere, *Tour*, pp. 274-5.

41. *Ibid.*, pp. 275, 288.

42. *Ibid.*, pp. 275-9.

43. Jackson, *Morocco,* pp. 269-281.

44. In his account Jackson refers to the sufferings of those people wrecked on the Barbary coast 'which no tongue can utter, no pen can accurately describe'. This phrase is very similar to one contained in a draft letter that Irving wrote to Matra. Irving describes how 'a sensible heart may in some degree feel that no pen or the tongue of a Cicero can express first a dreadfull shipwreck, then viewed by a party of naked savages with drawn knives expecting every moment to be deprived of a painfull existence and now consigned over to a slavery more detestable than death...'. In a letter to Captain Irving dated 27th September 1789 (Letter 21) Matra acknowledges receipt of a letter from him dated 10th August 1789. It is likely that this was based on the badly damaged draft held at the L.R.O., and may well have included this eloquent phrase. L.R.O., DDX 1126/16.

45. In a letter of 22nd October 1789, Matra informed Willlam Wyndham Grenville that 'by the last accounts the captain was very ill with a malignant fever', P.R.O. FO 52/8, 150-153.

46. P.R.O., FO 52/8, 172.

47. *Ibid.*, 184.
48. Lempriere, *Tour*, pp. 280-4.
49. P.R.O., FO 52/8, 190.
50. Schroeter, 'Merchants and pedlars of Essaouira', pp. 1-6, 15-19; El Mansour, *Morocco,* pp. 59-71.
51. Lempriere, *Tour*, pp. 86-9.
52. *Ibid.*, p. 87.
53. El Mansour, *Morocco*, pp. 19-26.
54. P.R.O., FO 52/8, 181-183.
55. Jackson, *Morocco*, pp. 258-263.
56. *Ibid.*, pp. 273-4, 279-281.
57. A view expressed in correspondence with Evan Nepean, 20th December 1789, P.R.O., FO 52/8, 181-183.
58. *Ibid.*. 160-161.
59. *Ibid.*, 177-179.
60. *Ibid.*, 180.
61. *Ibid.*, 182.
62. *Ibid.*, 190.
63. *Ibid.*, 182.
64. His name is variously spelt as Atall and Attar. *Ibid.*, 199.
65. *Ibid.*
66. *Ibid.*, 201.
67. *Ibid.*, 210.
68. A. Aspinall ed. *The correspondence of George Prince of Wales,*vol. II (London, 1964).
69. P.R.O., FO 52/8, 213.
70. Mawlay al-Yazid claimed the throne following the death of Sidi Muhammad, his father. He received extensive support from various influential groups, including the Berber tribes and the army, although as El Mansour points out the support dissipated quickly when he was unable to meet the diverse needs of his supporters. His death on 17th February 1792 created a new power struggle amongst a number of Sidi Muhammad's sons. El Mansour, *Morocco*, pp. 88-9, 101.
71. P.R.O., FO 52/8, 210.
72. *Ibid.*, 214, 221, 222.
73. *Ibid.*, 249.
74. El Mansour, *Morocco,* pp. 20, 88-9.
75. P.R.O., FO 52/8, 228-231.
76. El Mansour, *Morocco*, pp. 14-15, 89.
77. L.R.O., DDX 1126/1.

5. Freedom and return to England.
1. William Enfield describes Benns Garden chapel as one of three places of worship in Liverpool of the 'Presbyterian persuasion'. He comments that it is a 'neat and convenient building, and belongs to a numerous, flourishing and respectable society...'. William Enfield, *An essay towards the history of Liverpool* (Warrington, 1773), p. 47.

2. L.C.R.O., MF 1/32, RG. 4/1042.

3. Crow, *Memoirs*, pp. 3, 31, 92.

4. Boog Watson, 'Surgeons', pp. 210-211.

5. L.C.R.O., 614 INF 9/1.

6. Certificate of British Registry, M.M.M.A., C/EX/L/4, vol. 8, no. 133.

7. P.R.O., T64/286, 'An account of all vessels which have cleared for London, Bristol and Liverpool to Africa since the year 1788'.

8. *Williamson's Liverpool Advertiser*, January 10th, 1791.

9. P.R.O., BT 98/52, 31st July 1792.

10. The carpenter was an important crew member as he was required to erect structures for the control of the purchased slaves. Falconbridge, for example, refers to the construction of a 'barricado' of 'about eight feet in height ... made to project near two feet over the sides of the ship'. This structure 'serves to keep the different sexes apart; and as there are small holes in it, wherein blunderbusses are fixed, and sometimes a cannon, it is found very convenient for quelling the insurrections that now and then happen'. Falconbridge, *Slave trade*, pp. 5-7.

11. Minchinton, 'Triangular trade', p. 334.

12. H.L.R.O., HL Main Papers 28th June 1799, 28th July 1800.

13. P.R.O., BT 98/52, 31st July 1792; Richardson notes that it was usual for surgeons and other skilled crew members to return to the home port with the ship. Richardson, 'Costs of survival', p.189.

6. Conclusion.

1. Roger Anstey argues that '... received wisdom had so altered by the 1780s that educated men and the political nation, provided they had no direct interest in the slave system, would be likely to regard slavery and the slave trade as morally condemned, as no longer philosophically defensible'. In a more recent article Seymour Drescher examines Liverpool's response to the 'anti-slavery ideology which flowered toward the end of the eighteenth century...'. Roger Anstey, *The Atlantic slave trade and British abolition* (London, 1975), pp. 95-6; Seymour Drescher, 'The slaving capital of the world: Liverpool and national opinion in the age of abolition', *Slavery and Abolition*, vol. 9, no. 2 (September 1988), pp. 128-143.

2. Lempriere, *Tour*, pp. 275-6.

3. Falconbridge suggests that '... the surgeons employed in the Guinea trade are generally driven to engage in so disagreeable an employ by the confined state of their finances'. Falconbridge, *Slave trade*, p. 28.

4.*Jonathan Corncob*, an anonymous novel published in 1788, employs the phrase 'black cattle' to describe African slaves. C. Duncan Rice, 'Literary sources and the revolution in British attitudes to slavery', in Christine Bolt and Seymour Drescher ed., *Anti-slavery, religion and reform: essays in memory of Roger Anstey* (Folkestone, 1980), p. 326.

5. I am grateful to P. E. H. Hair for drawing this point to my attention; *The New Statistical Account of Scotland, vol. iv. Dumfries-Kircudbright-Wigston* (London, 1845), p. 20.

6. Duncan Rice, 'Literary sources', p. 319.

7. Falconbridge, *Slave trade*, p. 46; Tibbles, *Transatlantic slavery*, pp. 42, 60.

8. Crow, *Memoirs*, pp. 133, 176-7.

9. Sanderson, 'Liverpool delegates', p. 67.

10. Crow, *Memoirs*, pp. xvi, xviii, xxxiii, 170.

11. For a discussion of eighteenth century attitudes towards slavery see Anstey, *Atlantic slave trade*, pp. 91-153.

12. Patrick Manning, *Slavery and African life: occidental, oriental and African slave trades* (Cambridge, 1990), p. 122.

13. I would like to thank P.E.H. Hair for contributing a number of the ideas contained in this section.

14. L.R.O., DDX 1126/1.

15. *Ibid.*

16. Behrendt, 'Captains', pp. 111-115.

17. Langholm parish registers, 1668-1854, D.A.C., MF 67.

18. A painting of Thomas Golightly, mayor of Liverpool in 1772, is displayed in the Transatlantic Slavery Gallery at the Merseyside Maritime Museum. He is described as an alderman and senior member of the Council and Borough Treasurer between 1789 and 1820. See Tibbles, *Transatlantic slavery*, p. 74.

19. This section is based on information contained in an unpublished article by A.E. Truckell, 'Some 18th century transatlantic trade documents', a copy of which is deposited in D.A.C.

20. P.R.O., BT 98/52, 31st July 1792.

21. In a letter to James Irving III dated 17th March 1809 Frederick Hippins, a friend of the late Captain Irving, expressed his concern for Mrs. Tunstall's poor state of health. By 6th June 1809, Hippins conveys his sympathy on Irving's 'worthy Grandmother's departure'. Hippins corresponded with Toulmin and Copland of London regarding Mrs. Tunstall's pension. L.R.O., DDX 1126/37-39.

SECTION II:

COPY OF MR. JAMES IRVING'S JOURNAL WHEN SHIPWRECKED ON THE COAST OF BARBARY, 1789.

May 3rd 1789, at 4 a.m. weighed and sailed from Liverpool with a moderate favourable breeze[1] which ran us as far as Bardsey Isle in St. George's Channel, when it fell calm and veered into the southwest quarter blowing strong with thick rainy weather, in consequence whereof we bore away for St. Studwell road where we anchored on the 5th.[2] On the 7th sailed again, with a light breeze from the S.E. which failed again at noon, when we were boarded by a revenue cutter's boat, *Bardsey* ... bearing N.N.E. 29:06 N longitude per account 13: 20:W, or according to books and charts, a few leagues to the westward of Hegranza, the north eastern most of the Canaries.[3] The weather was clear with ~~with~~ a fresh breeze at north, but no prospect of land. Having duly considered our course and the compass steered by since we last took our departure, there was a strong presumption of our being to the westward of Hegranza. In consequence of that opinion, she was steered south per compass with a view to make Lancerota or Fortaventura before night. However, 6 p.m. arrived without any appearance of either, although we had run 34 miles. Thus baffled in our expectations, we were unanimously of opinion that an easterly current during our run from the Burlings had deceived us and that we were certainly to the eastward of the Canaries, however unaccountably it had happened.[4] Fully persuaded thereof we hauled up S.W.B.W. till sunset (7 p.m.), distance run 7 miles, and although we were favored with clear weather, could see no land from the masthead. We had then not a doubt of our being between the Canaries and the Barbary shore, and in order to avoid any probability of danger steered W.S.W. till 11 p.m., when the atmosphere that had hitherto been clear became a little cloudy and the breeze freshened.[5] The jibb and square sail were taken in, and the vessel steered W.B.S. The watch were also placed in the most proper stations for looking out. Midnight came without the least shadow of land or danger. The watch were relieved. The one betook themselves to sleep, the other to their respective stations as happy a ship's company as perhaps ever sailed but, alas, how fleeting was our felicity! I had not left the deck above ten minutes, when I heard the man at the helm say the water looked comically. Much alarmed at the expression, I jumped on deck and was met by a heavy broken sea that fell on board. We instantly endeavoured to haul the sheets aft and bring her to the wind which blew fresh at North or N.B.W., but the breakers fell on board so heavily and followed one another so quickly, that she soon lost headway and struck in the hollow of the sea so very hard that the rudder went away in a few seconds. She bounced with every wave so far to leeward that she lifted very little, but fell with such a shock that we expected every minute to find her part asunder or overset. In about ten minutes she filled, and the danger of over-setting being thereby increased we cut away the main-mast and hove everything of any weight that lay upon her deck overboard in order to prevent it. She lay for some time bow to sea, which considerably prevented her going to pieces (This journal was wrote by Mr. Irving, for his much loved brother-in-law, George Dalston Tunstall).[6]

I shall not attempt to explain our present shocking situation. You are capable of feeling what sensations occupied our minds when our vessel in which we were lately so happy, lay buffetted by heavy breakers, already buildged and full of water, no land or strand in view and three long tedious hours to pass before daybreak.[7] My late worthy friend Paisley's fate, immediately got root in my reflection.[8] Soon after she filled, something was descried to leeward. One supposed it land, another smooth water within the reef we had got upon. In a little time, however, we were all soon convinced that it was land, as the tide ebbed fast, which made it appear plainly. A raft was proposed whereon to take our chance, but as there was a probability of her sticking together till daylight we were all persuaded to stay on board.

Daylight long looked for at last appeared, and presented to us a low, flat, white sandy shore at the distance of a cables length. There was now only about four feet water alongside. In an hour we waded ashore, and took a view of it to the eastward and westward. Nothing but one uniform flat sand at high water and rugged rocks at low water, bounded by a high breaker and heavy surf.[9] Also examined the vessel's bottom and found her keel entirely beat off from stem to stern, two large holes in her starboard bilge and her water way and starboard side opened. All hopes of doing anything with her, or even putting to sea in the boat being vanished, we resolved to travel by land to the eastward in hopes of reaching Santa Crux or falling in with some hospitable inhabitants.[10] In consequence of this resolution, it was deemed proper to save the dollars if possible.[11] They were accordingly brought ashore and buried in the sand with some clothes, provisions, and water we had likewise brought ashore.

We set out about eight or nine in the morning, and in about an hour perceived the print of a human foot in the sand.[12] Before this discovery, we had believed the country uninhabited. We during the day passed several pieces of wreck and sometimes fell in with tracks made by the feet of camels, and amongst them the print of a dog's foot. All these discoveries confirmed the opinion of there being inhabitants in some part of the country, although you cannot conceive a more stricking picture of a desert and desolation. Nothing met your eye but a boundless sand driving before the northerly wind that accumulated in some places into impassable hills generally bare, although where the shore was steep and rocky the country inland produced several succulent seeds on which we imagined the cattle, the print of whose feet we had seen, must feed. With much difficulty we kept on foot till about six in the afternoon, exceedingly fatigued with travelling on loose sand, when we discovered a hanging or projecting cliff that formed a kind of cave. Here we resolved to lodge all night. Accordingly pieces wrecked vessels were gathered together and a fire made, around which we warmed ourselves, as the night was chilly.[13] We paired ourselves in order to keep a watch with a loaded blunderbuss that we had brought from the vessel to defend ourselves from wild beasts.[14]

May 28th. Started early in tolerable spirits having strong hopes of meeting with a river according to our chart, but alas! it was erroneous in this as well as in other respects. No river appeared and our stock of water was all expended, except about half a gallon that we were determined to save as a medicine should any of us be taken sick or unable to proceed. The shore was now become pretty high and formed by a perpendicular rock, the sea washing its bottom, so that we could no longer keep the sea on board, but travelled on top of the precipice when we had an extensive view of the country, which appeared a brown trackless sand with some herbs sprouting here and there.

About ten o'clock in the forenoon, perceived live animals at a great distance and soon after observed a flock of sheep, and almost at the same instant observed three people running from us over a small eminence that lay before us. We were all now big with anxiety, hopes, fears, resolutions and cowardice, a strange medley of ideas, some dropping astern, others pushing ahead. In this condition of mind three copper colored naked savages appeared before us on the top of the rising ground ahead of us, running at full speed and shouting hideously. They were followed by a tribe, some armed with long knives, others with muskets; you cannot conceive a scene more shocking, at least were you the victim on which it was practised. We were seized by the throats and our bundles instantly disappeared, as well as our neck handkerchiefs. They then cut and tore the clothes from our backs and so eager were they for the plunder that the weakest who in all probability would get a small share of it, attempted to stab us. I for my own part was struck at with a large dagger several times, and must have been terribly mangled had not a strong man defended me till he got wounded in the arm; the assailant then sheathed his weapon, and was allowed share of the plunder. During this scene of rapine, had frequent opportunity of seeing my unfortunate shipmates served in the same manner and fresh parties of Arabs coming from tents that lay at a greater distance, occasioned a repitition of the scene several times, till we were stripped almost naked.

We were then hurried away towards the tents that appeared at the distance of half a mile like mole-hills in the sand.[15] I complained of thirst and on my arrival at them was presented with about a quart of milk in a wooden dish. I drank it off at one draught and, although it contained beside the milk about a pound of sand, it was the most acceptable draught I ever drank. The men immediately left me in order to look for the vessel, and I was left under the charge of women. I now found time to reflect on my deplorable situation. My people were carried I knew not whither, all hopes of escaping cut off, and the distressing ignorance of my future fate wrought so forcibly upon me that my heart melted within me. My grief however, found vent at my eyes for a moment which considerably relieved the oppression I laboured under. In the afternoon, I observed one of the blacks standing at the door of a tent.[16] I ventured towards him, and enquired after the others. He informed me that the second mate and apprentice were at another tent about thirty yards distance. I went to visit them and found them asleep.[17] They had been more humanly handled by the banditte and retained the clothes they wore at leaving the wreck. They knew nothing of the others.[18] In this forlorn situation we passed the night under the eave of one of the tents.

May 29th. Was overhauled several times for money; every part of my body underwent the search. About noon to my infinite satisfaction, observed my mate and cousin coming from three or four tents about a quarter of a mile distant.[19] I believe there was scarcely ever a more agreeable meeting. They had each a flannel shirt and trousers left. One of them had been cut in the thigh when his pocket was cut off. They were also ignorant of the fate of the others who were missing. We each of us passed our conjectures respecting our situation. Many were our reasons to believe that if they spared our lives, it would only be to protract our miserable existance in a state of slavery. We however, resolved to use our joint endeavours to keep together and share the same fate. One of us had saved a Bible from which we selected some psalms and chapters suited to our forlorn situation, and received considerable comfort and benefit from reading them.[20] At night a separation again took place, contrary to our own desire. Each of us was forced to the tent he belonged to, almost famished. Late in the night by earnest intreaty I procured a drink of butter-milk and water, which was all I had tasted during the last four and twenty hours.

May 30th, was turned out at daybreak from among the sheep that went to graze. Hunger was now so keen that I was reduced almost to the last resource. After begging in the most suppliant manner, I procured some berries of a reddish color, almost of the size and taste of juniper. With these I filled the stomach without satisfying the appetite. About sunrise my mate and relation obtained leave to join us again, and about 10 a.m. were joined by the other five who were kept at another dowhar of tents, behind a rising sand at the distance of half a mile.[21] They had some pieces of biscuit which they shared with us, and a most affecting scene followed on the eating of it.

(The savages) after they had diverted themselves at our expense for the space of an hour, the five who visited us last were driven home (as I may call it) to the tents of the tyrants who possessed them. We who were left procured a pen and ink and some scraps of paper that we found in the sand where the vessel's papers had been, on which we wrote little certificates of our being in that country. They were distributed so that if any one of us at any time should ever get an opportunity to send one of them to Moggodore, or any other place where Christians resided, it might be the means of procuring our release.[22]

In the afternoon, the second mate and apprentice were delivered up to some strangers and marched away to the southward with them. This considerably increased our fears, as we knew of no civilized country in that direction. Towards evening we were sent to the seaside with each a skin on our backs in order to fetch water. Two or three women attended us and shewed us a hole amongst the rocks at high water, out of which we filled our bags with a very brackish water, and returned to the tents scarcely able through hunger and despondency to get one foot before the other. After dark they ground some barley by a hand mill and made some hasty-pudding, of which we received the leavings. There was now only three of us together and, after many entreaties on our side, they allowed us to spend the night together.

May 31st. Started at the usual time from our sandy couch and went with an intention of visiting our poor shipmates, but alas! they were not to be found. Our three black people told us that the whites (three in number) had set out very early without any of the Arabs, and that they had gone to the eastward.[23] This was a fresh pang and a paradox we could not solve. However, we were soon given to understand that they had been accompanied by their proprietors and were gone towards Morocco, where we supposed they would be sold for slaves.[24] Our Bible now was our only comfort.[25] How soothing is religion in affliction! We went to the seaside and gathered shellfish on which we made a very hearty meal, and thanked God most fervently that every source had not failed us.[26] In the afternoon whilst we strayed about amongst the sand, found several other pieces of the ship's papers and amongst the rest, our pass entire.[27] This we deemed a most grand acquisition. Two or three pieces of my surgeon's certificate also fell into our hands.[28]

June 1st. Nothing very particular occurred. Shellfish afforded a maintenance and the sand a bed. It was, after all, a difficult matter to exist. The savages, old and young, harrassed and distressed us most inhumanly by searching us for money, although they knew we had none. The men were by this time returned from the wreck, with several pieces of cloth and other articles of cargo.[29] The second mate and apprentice returned. They had been marched about twenty miles to the southward, but for what purpose they knew not, when they fell in with a number of tents where a man wrote something on a piece of paper with a stick, which was sent away by a messenger.

June 2nd. We passed most miserably. Early in the morning went to the seaside and gathered a few small shellfish, and on our return lighted a fire and roasted them. We had scarcely finished our repast when I perceived the man who claimed me as his property, coming towards us with hasty steps. He carried his musket and his wife followed him. He said something to the people of the tent and then turning hastily upon me, knocked me down and immediately uncased his gun. I was no sooner upon my legs, than he followed his blow and beckoned to march towards his tent, where a crowd of people were assembled. As I dreaded nothing so much as a separation, and supposing that was his intention, I resolved, should death be the consequence, to do what lay in my power to frustrate his intention. I therefore, ran past and seized hold of my companions. He endeavoured by many stripes and threats to force a separation without effect, and at last drove us all before him together, striking us as we passed on with the muzzle of his gun. We had no sooner got to the tent, than the whole party began their endeavours again, but my hold was similar to a death gripe. I confess I would rather have parted with life than have been taken away alone. Some of the party, I believed, sympathized for me and opposed the rude assaults of the others, so that they were soon divided into two parties; one for, the other averse to a separation. In a little time, my friends (so I may call them in this instance), prevailed. We were ordered to sit down with an assurance that no separation would be again attempted. They however, in the afternoon took an opportunity of driving the second mate and apprentice away, instead of me.

The agonizing state of mind we were then in can neither be conceived nor described, unless by one in a similar situation. In the evening we were made to understand that I, the chief mate and my relation were now left alone, (as for the two blacks who saw the treatment I received, took an opportunity during the tumult to steal away towards the sea unperceived and were no more heard of by us till many days after) should be taken to the Emperor of Morocco and sold, that if they could not obtain a hundred dollars a head for us they would cut our throats. This information, horrid as it may appear, considerably eased our minds and excited a hope of still obtaining our liberty and a sight of our dear native country. Our hope was founded on a probability of an ambassador being at the court of the Emperor of Morocco, and that when he heard his countrymen were on sale he would certainly for so trifling a sum, redeem us and return us to our country.

June 3rd, 4th, 5th, 6th, 7th and 8th. At the tents in a most deplorable situation. Our only comfort lay in our Bible, which was wantonly and most maliciously taken from us.[30] Our only employment was chiefly in fetching a load or two of water daily, and in the intermediate time gathering shellfish for our subsistence and endeavouring to keep ourselves clean and free from body vermin, which were innumerable. Every night at dark went as mendicants round the tents in hopes of obtaining something to eat or drink, but often without effect.

On the night of the 7th, we understood that in the morning we were to begin our journey towards the Sultan. This afforded us considerable pleasure. On the eighth our caravan began to move about nine in the morning. It consisted of seven men, one woman, six camels, and three slaves as their merchandise. About four in the afternoon came to a dowhar of tents, in number about forty, where our camels were unloaded and turned out to graze on the herbage which was more plentiful than in any part of the country we had seen. The people flocked around us and treated us most harshly. We craved a drink of water, but they buffetted us and spit in our faces. At last they consented to give us some, but obliged us to drink it out of our hats, as the dish would have been polluted had any of us touched it with our lips. The tent we stopped at was a school, and the master said prayers in the evening. It was evacuated before night, and we crept into it in hopes of enjoying the benefit of it during the night, but the inhospitable pedant soon dislodged us. The night was spent on the sand in the open air as usual. About night a draught of butter-milk and water was brought, which we drank off greedily. It made dinner, supper and breakfast.

June 9th. Got under weigh at daybreak, and in less than an hour halted at the edge of an extensive flat sand that appeared like a sea. Here the camels fed for half an hour, when they again set out and passed over several hills of accumulated sand that kept blowing before the wind like snow. One of the people acted as guide, running on the tops of the ridges and pointing out the most safe places for the camels to pass over. These hills formed a border girdle to the plain we descried when we halted. We were now got on to it, and its appearance at a distance beyond the visible horizon induced us to believe that the sea formed one side of it. It was perfectly level, as smooth as a table and incrusted over with a salt pellicle that cracked under our feet. In about four hours obtained a sight of the land on the eastward of it, and in another hour were entirely passed over. I am of opinion that its width was about 5 leagues. We were now arrived at the bottom of the hills that extended as far as we could see. Towards the east we fell into a beaten track, and passed over several ridges of sand. At about two in the afternoon crossed over a place that seemed to have been the bed of a river. There was only a little exceedingly salt stagnated water in it. On the east side of this, came to some tents on the side of a hill. Here we halted and staid for the night, but was severely harrassed by the young ones of both sexes. At night however, a large share of barley meal bargoe was given us.[31] Here it might be proper to observe, that our conductors had brought with them an old wooden dish from their tents for our use, as we observed that the people in every place would never again have used a dish that we had eat or drank out of, so great was their detestation and contempt of us.

June 10th. Soon after our setting out, we proceeded gradually towards the sea through an exceeding barren, stony, strubly country till we got within a mile of the sea at a high sand hill, which must be very remarkable when seen from the sea. It appeared with a saddle forming two hills. Here some of our convoy left us, and returned with some brackish water, which we supposed they had collected at high water mark by digging in the sand. A little to the eastward of these hills, they pointed out to us the place where a French vessel had been wrecked about three months before with a valuable cargo on board. They also said that the crew were with the Sultan. Some of them alighted and we were indulged with a ride on the camels. They are a most uneasy animal, but as we were exceedingly fatigued made a shift to hang on them for an hour or two, when they again mounted. The country was still exceedingly barren, the sea one league and the mountains another, the former to the northward and the latter to the southward of us.

At night we left the road and lodged between it and the sea on an open common, where there was tolerable good pasturage for the camels. A fire was lighted as usual, some stones were heated in it and afterwards immersed in a dish of water. They communicated a considerable degree of heat to it, when some barley meal was stirred into it, on which our conductors supped, their leavings fell as usual to our share. They afterwards forced us to gather some sticks and make a kind of barricade to screen them from the wind. Our situation was always in front of the place where they lay. Early in the night some noise was heard, on which they armed themselves and proceeded towards it. It was our opinion that they had seen nothing, although two of them did not return till the morning of June 11th, when the camels were accoutred and we proceeded along shore as before. In an hour or two came to another bed of a river, which was also dry. At the mouth of this the caravan also stopped and in a hole that was digged, we procured another bag of very brackish water. N.B. What I have called the bed of a river, was a deep cut in the land extending from the sea inland in a straight line. The sea at spring tides flows over a kind of sand bar and leaves a lake of salt-water about a foot deep. This water during the neap tides is nearly all absorbed and evaporated, and fills again on the next high spring tide. In the middle of this chasm, I suppose that during the rainy season a little brook may run. The banks of it were exceedingly steep, that we travelled almost a mile in the bottom of it before we could ascend to the other side. We proceeded along to the eastward as usual, between the sea and the ridge of mountains till the afternoon, when we inclined a little towards them and came to a small river of running water about five in the afternoon. This we supposed to be the Albagh river, as mentioned in the sea charts. It was very brackish and instead of using any of it, some stagnated rain water was taken out of a hole for use. Here one of the camels refused to pass over, although it was so shallow that we stepped over without filling our shoes. We found it necessary to drag him over by force, broadside foremost. We slept all night in a place where water had run during the rainy season. Supped on the same kind of mess as last night.

June 12th. Mustered a little before daybreak to get the camels rigged, and at daybreak started again. Scarcely able to walk with fatigue and despondency. We ascended out of the course of the river and proceeded along the side of the mountains to the eastward, as we judged by the sun, the sea in sight distant about three leagues. The country was still exceedingly barren but not so sandy, owing perhaps to our distance from and height above the sea. Saw several tents between us and the sea and large herds of camels and goats. Also met several people travelling in a contrary direction, some of whom enquired if there was any money or watches in the vessel. On our answering in the negative our conductors seemed much pleased, treated us with a drink of water and a ride and gave us to understand if we always behaved so they would treat us well, but if we should at any time, either on the journey or before the Sultan (as they styled the person, who they said they were carrying us to), divulge anything they would most assuredly cut our throats. About twelve p.m. met with a better dressed man than any we had yet seen. He was mount on a camel and carried a very long musket, ornamented with silver and ivory. After our conversation with our conductors, he enquired particularly for the master of the vessel, and spoke a word or two of

Spanish. He also turned back with us and conducted us over a ridge (here we lost sight of the sea) to a single tent where we halted. Here was a piece of cultivated ground and barley growing on it, and the proprietor was a son of one of our party. Here they employed us gathering barley during part of the afternoon, and at night we got some barley meal bargoe.[32] The man we met in the afternoon gave us some tobacco, and shewed us some other little kindnesses. The idea that we entertained of him was that he was an officer sent by the Government of Morocco to look after us and bring us to the King. We slept as usual in the open air amongst some loose straw.

June 13th. Were employed gleaning barley till about noon, when we mounted and proceeded to the N.N.E. Our new conductor took an opportunity to tell us something about a port where ships were, which he called Seveara. He also mentioned an English Consul, of the name of Hudson.[33] This intelligence afforded us much pleasure, as we thought there was some probability of his getting to hear of us and, if so, some steps might be taken to effect our deliverance. During this afternoon's travel saw several tents and much cattle, but no cultivated ground. In the evening halted, after having passed over several stony hills, at three tents that stood in a hollow, where was tolerable pasturage. Here, we and our conductors supped on some meal, berries and cold water and slept in the open air. The master of one of the tents with some courtesy brought a mat, on which he and the conductors seated themselves and conversed late. Were employed gathering sticks to make a fire.

June 14th. Travelled most of this day mounted. Saw several tents in the first part of the day, also two deer or antelopes. Travelled over several very extensive plains of fine soil, and saw several heaps of barley that had been cut down and gathered together. At one of the tents, halted in the afternoon where we found five or six people gathering the barley together. They only pull the ear from the straw and deposit it in handfulls. It is afterwards collected by the young ones of both sexes. Here they procured some water, made some dough and covered it up with some hot ashes till it was just heated through, when it was given us, and we proceeded on our journey. Came to a dowhar or hamlet of tents about the twilight. Here was vast numbers of camels and goats, and the pasturage tolerable. It was not grass but succulent herbs, which afforded food as well as drink. We were much at a loss to know how or where they procured water as it must be at least one whole day's journey to the sea, and the heat and drought was so intense, that the hills and valleys were parched like burnt ashes. We had never seen any pit or well, either here or in the sandy country. This night's situation was very cold on account of its elevation and being exposed to the northerly wind, but on account of our great fatigue having travelled a very long day's journey, sleep overcame us, although almost starved to death. Supper, some butter milk and meal. What a fine country this would be were it watered like Great Britain.

June 15th. Were on foot early and travelled till about noon. The soil and country similar to that we passed over yesterday. Saw several tents, much cultivated ground but no water or enclosure. We halted at a dowhar of tents, in number about thirty, six pitched in form of a crescent. My beard was by this time very long and troublesome; the person who we met three days ago procured me a pair of scissors, although unasked for, and desired me to use them on it. That action as it too much resembled the practice followed by slave traders gave us much trouble.[34] The people old and young were very curious to view us. Our conductors obtained a carpet on which they slept during the night. The ground as usual fell to our shares. Supped this night on a mess, we had never seen or tasted, cooscoosoo they called it. It is similar to sago, but made of barley meal and stewed dry in a cullender.

June 16th. Bilade, so our new conductor was called, set out with us (the others having stayed behind to procure horses to ride to town - as I may call it), and informed us that we should arrive at the place where the King resided that the mate and my relation would go to his house, and that I should lodge with himself and have food in plenty. This information excited fresh conjectures and much uneasiness. Willing however to put the best construction upon it, we supposed that as the maintenance of all of us in one house would be attended with some expense, more perhaps than one man could easily bear, that the dividing of us would lighten that expense on an individual. Bilade also assured us that the white people and one of the blacks, who had been marched from the tents in the desert on the 31st of May, were with the King, who he called Muley Abderhaman.[35] In about three hours we were overtaken by the other Arabs of our party, mounted on horse-back. At the same descried something like a fortification, which we supposed was on the frontier of the Emperor of Morocco. About ten in the forenoon passed a fine clear fresh water brook, issuing from a spring in a rocky imminence. Here we drank heartily and washed ourselves. It was the first we had seen since our shipwreck.

Early in the afternoon, arrived at the town where the King who we had so often heard of resided. I was taken to the house of our conductor, and my mate and relation went to the palace in a most distressed state of mind. The place was called Gulimeme alias Wadnoon.[36] It appears at a little distance like a fortification, as does every village in Barbary. The place we saw in the forenoon was another village of the same kind. They consist of a number of houses built of clay and closely connected with one another, so that the outside houses appear like the bastions and curtains of a fortified town. They are flat at the top with a battlement around them, appearing at a short distance like ambrazures. At night was served a most plentiful mess of cooscoosoo, and slept on the terrace upon the house-top.

June 17th. Was visited by my mate, who with much difficulty obtained liberty to see me under the escort of a stout black fellow. He informed me that he had seen the others and that they were employed in a garden belonging to the Prince to till and water it.[37] He also said that they had all been marched away, except the black man, he knew not whither and that the Negro and he had been employed in the garden ever since under the direction of a Mahometan Negro who beat them frequently. My mate obtained leave to spend the night with me.

June 18th, 19th, 20th and 21st. I spent in a most melancholy distracted state of mind, employed carrying water for the cattle etc., my bed the hard terrace and my food a supper of cooscoosoo. Saw no more of my shipmates, except the mate and black man working at a distance in the garden.

June 22nd. Was summoned before a company, of which my master made one. Here I was interrogated respecting the cargo of the vessel etc. They desired me to write, which I having done, they seemed pleased and told me I should go to Mogodore in a few days. This news dispelled many of the gloomy notions I entertained. One of the company took me out and told me he was to see me safe at Mogodore. From that time I looked upon him as my guardian angel. He also gave me some tobacco. About midnight I was alarmed with much stir in the house, and was soon turned out to proceed, as they said, towards Mogodore. The party consisted of about a dozen, mounted on horse and mules. I had many suspicious imaginations, as they proceeded in a direction that did not at all satisfy me.[38] On enquiry as to where they were going, they answered to Severa (Mogodore).

About three in the morning of the 23rd of June, halted at another village where we rested till daybreak, when we proceeded towards the N.E. through an extensive plain, surrounded by cloud-capped hills.[39] About noon I halted and refused proceeding further, unless they allowed me some food and drink. There were some houses at a little distance, where one of the party went and procured some parched barley meal and a little water, of which I made a meal. In the afternoon of June 23rd, I was unable to proceed through faintness. A Negro slave, who had been also purchased by my master, gave up about the same time.

Two of the party finding it impossible to get us forward, alighted from their mules and we were lifted upon them. We both rode about two hours, when we again alighted in order to descend into a valley that appeared below. In this valley we found a decent looking village at the principle house of which we stopped, it being sunset. This day's journey was the most fatiguing one I had hitherto travelled. The country during the latter part of the day was exceedingly mountainous, although a great deal was cultivated, and from the many cottages we had seen, I judged it to be populous. Although in this season all the rivulets between the mountains were dried up, except one only, in many places by the wayside we found tanks or cisterns containing fresh water that had been collected during the rainy season. The barley in many places was gathered in and thrown in heaps near their houses. I saw no other grain.

June 24th. Started from my stony couch half an hour before daybreak and proceeded in the same direction as yesterday, up one side of a mountain and down the other, passing many cottages and beds of rivers that were at present dried up by the excessive heat. The road in many places little better than a precipice. About 11 p.m. obtained the summit of the highest I had seen. In an extensive valley below I could perceive a town, where my new master (by name Sheick Brahim) informed me, the French people who had been shipwrecked some months before us, were in slavery. Their employment was chiefly in cultivating ground, and gathering in the crop. He also told me I was not going to Mogodore, but to a place called Tellin where he resided, where I must write to the Consul, who would send and purchase me and all the others.[40] In the meantime he promised to use me well.

About half past noon arrived at the town. The poor Frenchmen were sent for; distress and dejection were evident in their countenances. They informed me that their shipwreck happened on the 2nd or 3rd of January about 10 p.m., that the vessel was bilged, but that the natives gathered round them in great numbers, so that they had voluntarily surrendered. They also informed me that the current according to their opinion ran as strong as in the Gulf of Florida. They were bound for Senegal, with a cargo suited for the gum trade. I spent half an hour with them and shared of their allowance of cooscoosoo. I learned from them that they had repeatedly written to their Consul at Sallee, who had ordered them some clothes, also a trifling sum of money to be given them occasionally by a Jew who resided there, and that they had no immediate prospect of being redeemed from their deplorable situation.[41] This intelligence almost petrified me with misery. I could have died rather than devote my life to be spent in so abject a state, bereft of all Christian society, a slave to a savage race who despised and hated me for my belief. I would not proceed unless they allowed me to ride. This refusal procured for me two or three hard blows from the butt end of a musket. I was, however, allowed to mount a mule, and rode about half an hour, when they pulled me off and I took to my legs again during the afternoon's journey. We crossed a fine fresh water rivulet, where I again washed and refreshed myself.

At the close of day we got to Telling, my master's residence. Here were about 12 families of Jews, who were under my master's protection.[42] At the house of one of them, a fowl was boiled for me, and he told me in broken Spanish (of which I understood a little)[43] that I must reside with him at my master's expense, and that in the morning I must write to Mr. Hutchinson, the British Vice-Consul at Mogodore, informing him of my misfortune and situation as he (the Jew) had occasion to dispatch a courier for that place distant only about six day's journey. The Jew also assured me that the Vice-Consul would send and purchase me, and that myself and crew (if alive) would be returned to our native country. This intelligence quickened the small degree of hope that remained. I had, however, my fears concerning my poor fellow sufferers, as I knew not how they had been disposed of. In this situation, I betook myself to rest upon a rush mat, thankful to Providence for the prospects before me.

June the 25th. Wrote with a reed on coarse wrapping paper a long and plaintive letter to the Consul, and enclosed a list of the vessel's crew as they stood on the articles, requesting at the same time that he would take the earliest opportunity to inform Mr. Dawson of the fate of the *Anna*, his vessel.[44] I also mentioned my having saved the pass in the headband of my drawers, unknown to my tyrannical proprietors.[45] On account of the couriers being delayed, I wrote again on the 28th. to Messrs. Gwyn and Hutchinson, as I had been informed the latter was gone to Fez on business.

From this day till July 14th my time was spent most anxiously and impatiently, every hour seemed a day. At last, a long looked for letter came from the Vice Consul, inclosing one from a Mr. Atkinson Wynne. They informed me that the part of the coast where our vessel was wrecked, not being in the Emperor of Morocco's dominions, the unfortunate people who suffered shipwreck on that coast were seized by the Arabs or Moors inhabiting it and sold or otherwise disposed of as their interest or inclination directed.[46] The Consul also said that he would willingly send down a person to treat for our ransom, but that the Emperor did not allow any Christians to purchase shipwrecked people, that he took it upon himself as a compliment to the nation they belonged to, but he would immediately write to his Imperial Majesty as also to James M. Matra Esq., his Britannic Majesty's agent and Consul General in these dominions residing at Tangier, who would use every means in his power to effect our release, which, I might depend on would be soon.[47] He also desired me to keep up a correspondence with my people as much as possible, and to write him by every opportunity and inclose the pass in my first letter, in order that it might be sent home to the Admiralty, that the bond might be cancelled.[48]

All this flattering information afforded me some comfort, and I wrote the sum of the intelligence to my people, who I understood were employed at different places near Gulimeme in gardens belonging to Muley Abderhaman, who was an exiled son of the present Emperor. The second mate and apprentice were amissing, and I had many fears that they had either been detained in slavery in the desert or fallen a victim to the ferocity of the natives.[49] About this time I was informed by the Jew that I had been bought from Bilade at Gulimene by Sheik Brahim, my present master, for a hundred and thirty five ducats and that the least price he would accept was two hundred. Had I been master of the Indies, I would most cheerfully have parted with them for liberty, a priviledge so dear to Englishmen. From this day till the seventh or eighth of July, I lived tolerably and my labour was not severe, although most meanly servile. I wrought as a servant to the Jew, who was a kind of merchant. This service, though unavoidable, I cordially detested, as I discovered that the Jews in this country are little better than slaves to the Mahometans, their property, yea, their lives are at their disposal. Necessity, however, inculcated submission and resignation to my fate.

July the 8th. I received another letter from the Vice-Consul, inclosing another from Mr. Wynne. They contained little more than assurance of their friendly endeavours in our behalf, and that the time was near at hand when they hoped to see me at Mogodore. The Consul advised me to write to the Consul General and solicit his assistance. He also sent a piece of Oznaburg linen for frocks and trousers which the Jew was to get made up and sent to the others at Gulimene, and a cloak to my master to induce him to behave well to me.[50] I had also an order to take some other necessaries from the Jew. Mr. Wynne informed me that there was at that time in Mogodore a Moor of some rank who waited there for an opportunity to go as an ambassador to the Court of England, and that he had great hopes of our going along with him.

July 26th. Received a letter from my officers and people, in which they complained pitifully of the usage they received. They were beat most unmercifully and toiled hard from sunrise to sunset, that they were at that time all together except the second mate and apprentice who had been there for a week, but were marched away towards Morroco about a week before. My master, who was the bearer of this letter, brought with him James Drachm, one of the crew, who he had purchased.[51] About this time I was seized with a slight fever, which left me again in three days.

August the 1st. I received a most agreeable letter from the Vice Consul informing me that the second mate and apprentice were arrived at Morocco in health, and that he expected every day to see them at Mogodore and that the Emperor had given orders to one Sintob Ben Attar to go and redeem us all and take us to Morrocco. The Vice-Consul also wrote to my master that he would pay him the sum he demanded for me and the others immediately on our being brought to Mogodore.[52] But he, instead of accepting his offer, collected all the money he could and went in two or three days afterwards to Gulimene in order to purchase as many of the others as his purse would effect. In a week he returned with William Brown, John Richards, and Jack Peters, three others of the crew, and desired me to write the Consul that our prices were now augmented to nine hundred dollars for the five in his possession, and Muley Abderhaman would not take less for the four with him than seven hundred dollars.[53] This declaration afforded fresh cause of grief and misery to us. We languished and pined in sorrow, dreading an addition to our price at every advance that might be offered for us.

Early in September I experienced another attack of fever, which rendered me delirious during the hot stage of the paroxism which seized me every day. I wrote to Mogodore for medicine and received some, which was all the Consul could procure of what I wanted.[54] Judge of my situation, my bed the hard earth and my drink from the cistern. My poor shipmates ministered unto me, and gave me all the help and assistance in their power. In this condition I languished for forty days, when John Richards, William Brown and Jack Peters were redeemed and taken away by some officers of the Emperor. James Drachm alone remained, but the poor man felt the separation so sensibly that in two days afterwards he sickened and in twelve days more paid the debt of nature.[55] My endeavours in his behalf so exhausted me that I suffered a relapse, and continued in a weak situation scarcely able to help myself till the last day of November when heaven be praised, three horsemen belonging to Prince Absolam, who at that time resided at Tarradant about three days' journey distant, arrived at the house of my master and with much difficulty purchased me for two hundred dollars.[56] In the intermediate time, I received many letters from the Vice-Consul and one from the Consul General all informing me how matters went on and exhorting me to bear up under my afflictions for the day of my redemption would certainly come soon. The Consul-General procured a surgeon from Gibraltar, and sent him to attend this Prince for a defect of sight.[57] This office to the Prince conduced considerably to my being redeemed.[58] Early in October, while at Telling, I received information that the others at Gulimene had been ransomed and marched towards Morocco. This piece of service was also done us by the same

Prince, who was constantly stimulated on by the Vice Consul's letters and presents.[59]

December the 1st. Left Telling, which I may deem one of the happiest days of my life. The people who purchased me procured a mule on which I and one of the party was mounted, and that night I got into the dominions of the Emperor and staid all night at the house of an alcaide, or officer, about twenty miles to the south eastward of Agadire or Santa Creuz.[60] I was still in a very poor state of health, and the motion of the mule so disordered me that I was scarcely able to turn myself, but the fair prospect of a termination of my slavery and imprisonment buoyed me up and supported me. I was kindly entertained by my convoy, who assured me I should soon see my native country.

December 3rd. Got to Tarradant, the most southerly town or city in the dominions of the Emperor. It lies nearly east from Santa Cruz and is a walled town of tolerable extent situated in the centre of a fruitful valley, well watered by a large river. Here are many fine gardens and a royal palace.[61] In the afternoon I was taken before the Prince, where I was much surprised to see the deference and respect that was shown him. I expected to find him only one degree removed from a savage as all the other Moors or Arabs are, but I found him seated in an ante-chamber or rather portico, and the avenue to it formed by two rows of his bodyguard or domestics who bowed frequently and whenever he deigned to say anything, they all answered "Nama Cidi", that is, "Yes, your Majesty", and ran to execute his orders with a cheerful alacrity.[62] Among his officers was one who understood a little English. He interrogated me respecting my country, the place I was wrecked and the station I filled on board the vessel. When I was carried from his presence, where I as well as every Moor of whatever rank had stood barefooted, I omitted mentioning that the surgeon who attended him from Gibraltar, (but who had been ordered to Morocco by the Emperor) had informed him of my having been bred to physic. This he did to induce the Prince to send and redeem me, in order that I might attend him while the other was absent.[63]

As soon as he had issued all his orders, he withdrew to an inner apartment, when I was again ordered in and questioned respecting his complaint. He sat upon a bed like a tailor upon his shopboard with a cushion under each knee. His dress was rich and graceful. His menial servants stood, and the chief scribe with other grandees sat at some distance from him on a carpet. He was served with a cup of coffee poured from a gold pot, and the rest of the service was of plate. The chambers were large and spacious, the wall was hung round with a kind of tapestry and the floor tiled with various coloured tiles arranged in different figures and covered with a rich Turkey carpet.[64] I was with him about half an hour, when I was dismissed with a promise that he would new clothe me and that I must follow a person who he ordered with me to a Jew's house where I would find maintenance, and that he would send for me next morning.[65] This however, happily for me he did not, as the slow fever that still preyed upon me obliged me to lie all day.

Next day I was sent for and my opinion and advice was again taken respecting his disease. From that time till the 26th current I visited him daily, as also the governors and several other seraglios or harems where no Moor was admitted.[66] I met with a Spanish renegade who stood linguist on all occasions, but stood without the door and explained what I said to those within. During this time I was most grievously harassed by the uncivilized Moors who, hearing that I was a doctor, flocked around me in the streets and with outstretched hands begged I would examine their pulses, and so great was their ignorance that they believed I could by so doing not only discover their complaints but cure them.[67] While I remained here, I met with a Frenchman who kept a little shop and by the Vice-Consul's order I received some necessaries from him. He told me that all my people had been there, but were immediately sent to the Emperor at Morocco where they remained, as there was some disagreement between the Emperor and the Court of England.[68] From this place I wrote the Vice Consul and also my friends in England.[69]

December the 26th. The Prince having received orders from his father to come to Morocco, I made one of his train, having received from him a coat, waistcoat, trousers and five ducats in money, with which I purchased some few other necessaries.[70] About noon, the caravan moved from the palace, in number about three hundred, all mounted on horses, camels and mules.[71] I was placed upon a loaded mule and we proceeded across the plain towards the foot of Mount Atlas, one of the highest mountains in the universe. About eight at night, we pitched our tents at the bottom of the mountains. The cattle were unloaded, and fires lighted before each tent as the nights were very cold. At daybreak the Prince with the grandees and bodyguard, mounted and began to ascend by a zig-zag road.[72] The baggage mules followed immediately after. About noon we had got to the top, which was covered with ice and snow and in the valley below tall trees could not be distinguished, although the place where we passed over was the lowest part of the whole chain. To the right of us the mountain appeared double the height. It was at that place we continued descending till sunset, when the tents were again pitched and we passed the night as before. During our descent we passed several brooks of fine water that drizzled down from the summit, and in the evening saw several villages. I lodged in the steward's tent and was plentifully supplied with provisions by the Prince's orders, but was almost starved to death owing to my want of bedding and sickly condition.

28th December. Struck the tents at daybreak, and soon after crossed a fine river of fresh water. Our course was most of this day to the N.E. over several high hills and stony roads. About four in the afternoon the tents were pitched near a village, where was a fresh water brook.

On the 29th proceeding again at daybreak and sunrise in the same direction as yesterday. The road very stony and mountainous, and about noon got clear of the chain of mountains which make a part of Atlas and came into the plain where Morocco stands.[73] At sunset the tents were pitched by the side of a river, some villages at a little distance.

On the 30th were all mounted about sunrise, and proceeded to the eastward over a flat, dry country. During this day's travel crossed two or three brooks that arose from the mountain, and ran across the plain towards the north. Here was much cultivated ground and many people ploughing, some with two acres, some with two camels and others with bullocks. About five in the afternoon passed through a pleasant village where were many gardens and olive trees. About half a mile to the eastward of it pitched our tents. This night whilst I lay asleep, a person called and presented me with a letter from Mr. Hutchinson informing me of his having heard that I was at Tarradant. He had sent some clothes by the bearer. The man said I could not get them till we got to Morocco, which would be next day, where they would all be delivered to me safe.[74]

On the 31st moved about the usual time, and in about two hours got sight of the highest steeple in the city of Morocco distant about twenty miles, and soon after crossed several rivers from which canals were cut to water the intervening country.[75] About three in the afternoon got to the outside of the walls, where stood the surgeon who had been at Tarradant. He was going to pay his court to the Prince.[76] Here we alighted. The Prince was admitted at a back gate to his palace. The guards fired a volley, and soon after I was visited by my officers and people. It was a most joyful interview. We had not seen one another for almost seven months.[77] They informed me how they were situated. The Emperor allowed them sixpence a day. They lodged at a Jew's house at the expense of the British Vice-Consul, and had no prospect of being released from their captivity.[78] I was pleased to see them tolerably well clothed. The Vice Consul had sent them supplies of that kind.[79] I obtained leave to go with the surgeon and the others to their lodgings. The greatest part of the night was spent in reciting our hardships past and present.[80]

January the 1st. I received my parcel from the Moor that had been sent me from the Vice Consul. On opening it I found a complete suit of common clothes, and amongst the rest one of my own shirts that had ~~had~~ been carried from the wreck and sold at Mogodore to the Vice Consul. He knew it, therefore purchased and sent it to me.[81] From this time till the 17th I lived with my people, and had two audiences of the Emperor. I understood from him that we would not be set at liberty till our Court should think proper to send an ambassador, that some difficulties had subsisted between the Courts might be settled.[82]

On the 16th were informed that his Majesty intended sending us a Mr. Layton, and (go) to the Vice Consul at Mogodore where we should receive the same allowance as we did here, but should not be allowed to leave the country till he gave orders for so doing.[83]

January the 18th. Mules were prepared for us and we set out in a party under a guard in order to proceed to Mogodore,[84] and on the 20th in the afternoon arrived there[85] and were immediately visited by our good Consul who took us to his house and provided dinner for us. He also procured a room for us.[86] Mr. Layton continued paying the sixpence a day by the Emperor's order.[87] Our situation now may appear to many as tolerably comfortable, but when they are informed that the room we lodged in was no better than a cellar without a window or any kind of furniture.[88] The ground made our bed, and we covered ourselves with a kind of blanket called a haique, one being given to each of us by the Vice Consul, but what tendered most of all to our dejection and unhappiness was the poor prospect, or rather no prospect, of our ever obtaining our precious liberty.[89] We had never heard of, or from, any of our friends at home and the infernal government under whose clutches we were inthralled, together with the insulting, abusive and domineering conduct of the barbarians, we had few comfortable moments.[90]

About the 20th of April we received information of the death of the Emperor Sede Mahomet.[91] This intelligence threw the whole country into an uproar. The town was fortified on the land side and cannon were transported from the batteries that commanded the sea to the land side of it, and every inhabitant wore arms and kept watch as the Barbs from the mountains were daily expected to plunder the town as Government was suspended and no one knew who should succeed to the throne.[92] Muley Al Jezid was at last established and proclaimed, and in a few weeks all was quiet again.[93] During this disturbance, we concerted a plan for our escape. I made it to get on board of the vessels in the bay, but no one would consent to carry us off. This was by some means or other carried to the Governor who placed guards over us, and no one was allowed to pass the threshold of the door, myself excepted, who was permitted to go and purchase provisions etc. I complained to the Vice Consul who procured a tolerable alteration for the officers and we went by turns to market, but never were permitted to pass the town gates till the last week of July when the sentries were taken off, and in two or three days a new Emperor's letter to the Governor (through the medium of our Consul General) was received when we were all summoned before him and formally delivered up to the Vice Consul as British subjects at his disposal.[94] Let the sympathising and sensible heart judge of our joyful feelings on this happy occasion. Our good Vice Consul bountifully enabled us to make merry, and the evening was spent in conviviality.[95]

August 1st. We were distributed on board the different English vessels in the bay in order to take our passage to England, and bare and penniless as we were, we began to anticipate better days.[96] Two went on board the sloop *Charlotte*, Captain William Davis.[97] Two others on board the *Tryal*, Captain Plumb Balding.[98] Two were shipped on board as seamen in the brig *Bacchus*, Captain Prouting, and my two mates, surgeon and self went also on board of her as passengers, and on the twenty fourth of September sailed from Mogodore Bay with a cordial prayer that we might never again visit those barbarous regions in a similar predicament.[99]

October the twenty sixth, put into Dartmouth with a foul wind and short of provisions.[100]

JOURNAL: Notes.

1. *Williamson's Liverpool Advertiser* of 18th May 1789 recorded that the '*Ann*, Irving' sailed on 3rd May 1789. See Letter 9.
2. Bardsey Island lies to the south west of Aberdaron off the Lleyn Peninsula, North Wales. 'St. Studwell road' is almost certainly St. Tudwal's Roads, also off the Lleyn Peninsula, near Abersoch.
3. 'Alegranza' is an island marked on the navigational chart of 1794, directly to the north of 'Lancerota'. M.M.M.A., OA. 1866. Atlas of Charts, 1794. This section seems to provide an incomplete account of the voyage as it implies that the *Anna* reached the Canary Islands on the same day as sailing from 'St. Studwell road'. I therefore strongly suspect that there is a missing section between the words 'revenue cutter's boat' and 'bearing N.N.E. 29:06 N. longitude per account 13:20 W'.
4. The timing of the voyage is confusing. If a short section of the journal has been accidently left out in transcription this could account for the period between 7th May and their shipwreck in the early hours of 27th May 1789.

5. This confusion about location can be compared with the experience of the slave captain John Newton during a voyage on the *Duke of Argyle*. Martin and Spurrell, *Journal of a slave trader,* pp. 8-9.

6. George Dalston Tunstall was the brother of Mary Irving née Tunstall. A number of letters indicate that Irving regarded him with affection.

7. In a draft letter to James Matra, Consul General to Morocco, Irving explained that 'I was lately master of the schooner *Anna* of and from Liverpool bound to the Gold Coast of Africa, but was carried on by a strong current and wrecked on the 27th May last ... south of Forturventura...' L.R.O., DDX 1126/16.

8. The editor is unable to expand upon this reference.

9. *Lloyd's List* of 29th September 1789 reported that 'the *Ann*, Irving from Leverpool to Guinea, is wrecked at Uld Nun; the cargo plundered and crew made slaves'. A navigational chart of 1794 indicates that 'Nun' was located on the north-western coast of Africa, opposite the Canary Islands, and in present day maps is recorded as 'Noun' (see Map 4). M.M.M.A., OA. 1866., Atlas of Charts, 1794.

10. The navigational chart of 1794 indicates that Santa Cruz was located on the coast to the north of the position of their shipwreck. Jackson indicates that it was also known as Agadir. Jackson, *Morocco,* p. xi.

11. In the first letter that Captain Irving sent to John Hutchison, the British Vice-Consul to Morocco, he explained that the cargo of the *Anna* included 'India, Manchester and hardware goods with about 20 tons salt, which was washed out. She had also 1000 dollars on board, all of which fell into the hands of the Arabs' (see Letter 10). As the *Anna* was a slaving vessel, this cargo was to be used for bartering for slaves. P.R.O., FO 52/9, 115-116.

12. Reminiscent of Daniel Defoe's *Robinson Crusoe*, a work with which Irving was probably familiar. At first, this almost fictional quality led me to doubt the authenticity of this copy journal, but as highlighted in the preface there is a great deal of independent evidence which confirms the account.

13. In his early 19th century *Account of the Empire of Morocco*, James Grey Jackson comments on 'this deceitful coast which has in times past and now continues to enveigle ships to destruction'. Jackson, *Morocco*, p.271.

14. It was usual for slave traders to be armed in case of riot amongst the slaves. Falconbridge, a former surgeon in the trade, makes reference to blunderbusses inserted into small holes in a partition across the ship which 'is found very convenient for quelling the insurrections that now and then happen'. Falconbridge, *Slave trade*, p.6.

15. The comparison of the tents with mole-hills is effective. Lempriere who visited Morocco later that year described how 'the form of an Arab tent is in some degree similar to a tomb, or the keel of a ship reversed. They are dyed black, are broad, and very low'. Lempriere, *Tour*, p. 34.

16. The crew list which Irving supplied to Hutchison in his first letter of 24th June 1789 indicates that three crew members were 'Portuguese blacks' named Silvin Buckle, James Drachen and Jack Peters (Letter 10).

17. The same crew list indicates that the second mate, M. Francis Dawson, was a nephew of John Dawson, the merchant. The name of the apprentice was Samuel Beeley (Letter 10).

18. Ten crew members were listed in addition to James Irving, the captain.

19. The crew list indicates that the first mate was John Clegg. The captain's cousin and namesake was listed as ship's surgeon (Letter 10).

20. The words 'Bible', 'psalms' and 'chapters' are enlarged and embellished. This has been reproduced by the person who transcribed this copy of his journal. This is a practice that Irving employed in a number of letters to his wife, and provides a further indication of the authenticity of the journal. L.R.O., DDX 1126/1, /6.

21. 'Douhar'. An encampment of tents. Lempriere, *Tour*, pp. 34-6.

22. Mogodore (or Essaouira to use the Arabic name) is a seaport town on the Atlantic coast of Morocco founded in 1764 by Sidi Muhammad.

23. The letter to Hutchison includes three 'Portuguese blacks' in a list of crew members. Excluding the captain, first mate, second mate, surgeon and apprentice left three seamen: Joseph Pearson, William Brown and John Richards. P.R.O., FO 52/9, 115-116.

24. The city of Morocco is now known as Marrakech.

25. As Irving's son was later baptised at Benns Garden chapel in Liverpool it is likely that he worshipped at this Presbyterian chapel, which is logical given his Scottish background. William Enfield commented that it is a 'neat and convenient building, and belongs to a numerous, flourishing and respectable society'. Enfield, *Liverpool*, p.47.

26. The word 'God' is enlarged and embellished.

27. This refers to the Mediterranean Pass which was issued by the Admiralty Office to protect shipping from the activities of Barbary corsairs or pirates. The register of passes records that pass number 7469 was issued to James Irving, master of the *Anna* bound to Africa and America at Liverpool on 16th April 1789. P.R.O., ADM 7/109, ADM 7/108.

28. The Dolben Act of 1788 stipulated that there should be at least one surgeon on board a slave ship with a 'certificate of his having passed his examination at Surgeons Hall'. In the examinations book of the Company of Surgeons, the predecessor of the Royal College of Surgeons of England, James Irving is bracketed together with four other individuals who were all passed as 'Surgeons to African ships' on 2nd April 1789. I am grateful for this information supplied in correspondence by Miss Glen Jones, Librarian, the Royal College of Surgeons of England; 'An Act to regulate, for a limited time, the shipping and carrying of slaves in British vessels from the coast of Africa', Donnan, *History of the slave trade*, pp. 582-9.

29. See above, note 11.

30. The word 'Bible' is enlarged and embellished.

31. Irving comments on the cultivation of barley on a number of occasions.

32. For a discussion of the agrarian economy of Morocco see El Mansour, *Morocco*, pp. 35-38.

33. Lempriere refers to 'Mogodore, so named by Europeans and Suera by the Moors...', Lempriere, *Tour*, p. 86; Hudson is undoubtedly a reference to John Hutchison, British Vice-Consul at Mogodore.

34. Prior to attaining his first captaincy, Irving completed at least five slaving voyages between July 1783 and January 1789. As surgeon he would have accompanied the captain and would have been required to examine the slaves carefully before purchase.

35. Mawlay 'Abd. al-Rahman was the exiled son of Sidi Muhammad b. 'Abd. Allah,

Emperor of Morocco between 1757 and 1790. In exile, he established independent
political control in the district known as the Sous which formed part of the southern
territories. El Mansour, *Morocco*, pp. 89, 96.

36. The present day settlement of Goulimine is located to the south of Taroudant, Agadir
and the Anti-Atlas mountain range. It is currently featured as a tourist attraction in a
number of holiday brochures (see Map 4).

37. This is consistent with information Irving supplied to Hutchison. In a letter dated 24th
June 1789 he points out that a number of his crew members 'are with the Muley
Abdrahman, at Gulimeme working while the sun shines in the open field' (Letter 10).
P.R.O., FO 52/9, 115-116.

38. This corresponds with information in the letter of 24th June, a copy of which survives
amongst consular papers in the P.R.O. Irving explained that 'when I set out was told that
they were going directly to you, but I find shall be detained here till your answer
determine our fate'. *Ibid.*

39. This description of his journey from Goulimine to 'Tellin' indicates that he was
referring to the Anti-Atlas and Sirwa mountains with peaks of between 7,000 and 10,000
feet. The Moroccan Tourist Board describes the Anti-Atlas as 'the beginning of the
mountains of the Sahara, stark and arid with sombre outcrops, but interspersed with
verdant oases'; *Morocco. Mountains and Valleys*, pp. 8-9.

40. Variously spelt by Irving as 'Telling', 'Teilin' and 'Tellin', this was probably a very
small settlement as it is not marked on contemporary or modern-day maps. In a letter to
his wife dated 1st August 1789, he indicated that his crew at Goulimine was 'about thirty
miles from this place' (Letter 16). In a journal entry for 30th November 1789, Irving
records that he was a three day journey from Taroudant. Taken together, the various
references suggest that 'Telling' lay about thirty miles north-east of Goulimine close to
the coastal end of the Anti-Atlas mountains (see Map 4).

41. In the letter surviving amongst consular papers in the P.R.O., Irving comments that
'As I passed from Gulimeme hitherward, just got leave to speak to the Frenchmen' (Letter
10). P.R.O., FO 52/9, 115-116.

42. Jews were regarded as inferior members of society who were not permitted to own
land. Their 'dhimma' status was signified by the compulsion to wear distinctive dress. El
Mansour, *Morocco*, pp. 14-16.

43. Irving may have acquired a familiarity with the language during the two slaving
voyages on the *Princess Royal* between 1787 and 1789 to Cuba in the Spanish West
Indies. P.R.O., BT 98/48, 19th January 1788; BT 98/49, 2nd March 1789.

44. This refers to the letter Irving sent to Hutchison, a copy of which survives amongst
the papers of James M. Matra, Consul General to Morocco. In the letter Irving apologises
for the 'shamefull scrawl done with a reed' (see Letter 10).

45. The pass had furnished no protection from the nomadic desert tribes.

46. James Grey Jackson observed that 'the district of Wedinoon ... being thus only
nominally in his dominions is another impediment to the redemption of the mariners who
happen to be shipwrecked about Wedinoon...', Jackson, *Morocco*, pp. 276-277.

47. Matra had received news of their circumstances by 21st July as he wrote to the
Secretary of State's office to inform them of 'the loss of the schooner *Anna*.' (Letter 13).

48. In a letter of 21st July 1789, Hutchison informs Irving 'I have received the pass safe, and it shall be transmitted to the Admiralty Office in order that the bond for it may be cancelled' (Letter 14).

49. The comments on the location of his crew members correspond with the letter found amongst Matra's consular papers. In this letter Irving pointed out that 'my mate, surgeon and six men are with the Muley Abdrahman, at Gulimeme, working while the sun shines in the open field. My second mate and an apprentice are somewhere else in the country' (Letter 10). P.R.O., FO 52/9, 115-116.

50. This description broadly corresponds with a letter from Hutchison dated [?]21st July 1789 (see Letter 14), although the dates do not match exactly. If the journal was written in retrospect, this may explain the discrepancy.

51. In a letter to Hutchison dated 2nd August 1789, a copy of which survives amongst consular papers in the P.R.O., Irving points out that 'my master arrived here last night from Gulimeme where he hath been these 18 days past, and hath brought with him one of the blacks' (see Letter 17). P.R.O., FO 52/9, 117.

52. This description corresponds with the contents of a letter from Hutchison dated 13th August 1789 (see Letter 18).

53. This was an increase of 400 dollars on the price which Irving had reported to Hutchison in his letter of 2nd August (see Letter 17).

54. In a letter to Irving dated 1st November 1789, Hutchison noted that 'I am glad you received the medecines and that your fever has in a manner left you' (see Letter 23).

55. A report later written by Matra confirms that it was James Drachen who died in captivity, as his is the only name missing from a crew list which he sent to Whitehall in December 1789. P.R.O., FO 52/8, 177-180.

56. In a letter to the Secretary of State's office dated 19th December 1789, Matra points out that 'Doctor Lempriere in a letter to me of the 24 hour says Prince Abslem that morning had sent off a party to bring in Captain Irving...'. P.R.O., FO 52/8, 177-178.

57, In a letter dated 24th September 1789, Matra informed the Secretary of State's department that 'I have at last procured a good doctor for the Prince who goes tomorrow to Mogodore, a favour that will make him zealous to procure the seamen...'. P.R.O., FO 52/8, 144.

58. A view also expressed by Matra in correspondence. *Ibid.*, 184.

59. Lempriere comments that late in October 1789 a number of the crew members of the *Anna* passed through Taroudant 'in their way to the metropolis'. Lempriere, *Tour*, p. 132.

60. 'Alcaide' refers to the governor of a town. Lempriere, *Tour*, p. 17.

61. Lempriere commented that a number of lofty palm or date trees 'which are intermixed with, and overlook the houses' gave the town 'a very rural appearance'. Lempriere, *Tour*, pp. 159-160; the Moroccan Tourist Board describes present day Taroudant as 'elegant and imposing,with gardens enclosed, as is the town, by ramparts and walls'.

62. Lempriere comments that the Prince was aged about 35. It is unlikely that the extremely unfavourable description he provides of the Prince's appearance and character is based on an objective assessment. Lempriere, *Tour*, pp. 151-3.

63. This corresponds directly with Lempriere's account. *Ibid.*, pp. 169-170.

64. This corresponds closely with Lempriere's description of the palace. *Ibid.*, pp. 123-129.

65. This may have been 'the habitation of the Prince's principal Jew...' where Lempriere had previously been lodged. *Ibid.*, pp. 129-130.

66. Lempriere was also required to offer medical advice to the women in the Prince's harem. *Ibid*, pp. 139-146.

67. Lempriere also complained about the same problem. *Ibid.*, p. 138.

68. In a letter to Irving dated 1st November 1789, Hutchison commented that some of his crew members who passed through Taroudant 'received some little necessaries from a Frenchman at that place by my directions, and were to set out next day for Morocco where they are no doubt arrived' (Letter 23).

69. There are no surviving letters written by Irving in December 1789.

70. In a letter to Irving dated 11th January 1790, Hutchison commented that he was 'very glad to see that the Prince was so considerate as to supply you with some necessary cloathing' (Letter 25).

71. Lempriere noted that Irving travelled with Mawlay 'Abd. al Salam to Morocco [Marrakech]. Lempriere, *Tour*, p. 274.

72. This sounded a suprisingly modern phrase, but reference to the *Concise Oxford English Dictionary* confirmed its eighteenth century usage.

73. Marrakech is situated to the north of the High Atlas mountain range. Jackson estimated its population at 270,000 and commented that it is 'situated in a fruitful plain' with the 'snow-topped mountains of Atlas in the background...'. Jackson, *Morocco*, pp. 57-65.

74. This reference is confirmed in a letter dated 11th January 1790, in which Hutchison refers to sending the captain a parcel of clothes (see Letter 25).

75. The 'steeple' may refer to the high square tower of a mosque described by Jackson as the Lantern Tower. Jackson, *Morocco*, p. 61.

76. Lempriere provides a fuller account of this meeting. Lempriere, *Tour,* pp. 274-5.

77. Irving is clearly referring to the date of their original capture at the end of May 1789.

78. This corresponds with information contained in Hutchison's letter of 11th January 1790 (see Letter 25).

79. In a letter to the Secretary of State's office dated 4th December 1789, Matra reported that 'as they came perfectly naked, cloaths are by my direction made at Mogodore for them, and I have given such directions to my agents as shall keep them supplied in case the Emperor's orders in their favour be not properly attended to...'. P.R.O., FO 52/8, 172.

80. Judging by Lempriere's comments, the two surgeons became quite well acquainted in the period spent in Marrakech. Lempriere, *Tour*, pp. 274, 288.

81. See above, note 74.

82. In a letter to his wife, dated 31st January 1790, he refers to a meeting with the Emperor (Letter 27).

83. One of the reasons why Matra negotiated for the transfer of the men to Mogodore was that he considered it 'much safer from the first effects of a commotion in case of a revolt in the country'. P.R.O., FO 52/8, 189, 190.

84. In a letter to the Secretary of State's office dated 14th February 1790 Matra reported that they had 'all safely arrived' at Mogodore. He noted that 'His Imperial Majesty sent his mules down with them giving orders that the hire of them should be paid into his Treasury at that place'. P.R.O., FO 52/8, 190.

85. Captain Irving's first letter to his wife from Mogodore is dated 31st January 1790 (Letter 27).

86. In a letter to his wife dated 31st January 1790 he commented that 'Our humane consull Mr. Hutchison ... supplys us with cloaths and the necessarys of life...' (Letter 27).

87. Jackson describes Mr. A. Layton as a British merchant at Mogodore and 'the chief partner in a house of considerable capital and respectability', Jackson, *Morocco*, pp. 263-5.

88. Jackson noted that '... the houses having few windows towards the street, they have a sombre appearance'. *Ibid.*, p. 51.

89. Letters written by Matra, Hutchison and Irving tend to confirm James Grey Jackson's observation on 'the tardiness ... of diplomacy'. *Ibid.*, p. 273.

90. Mr. Robson who tried to forward letters to Captain Irving commented that 'since Mr. Irving has been at Mogodore, Mrs. Irving has heard from him often and has as often wrote, as well as many more of his friends here but he never has received any of the letters though they have been sent from the Secretary of State's office to the Consul at Mogodore' (Letter 33).

91. On 15th April 1790, Matra reported to the Secretary of State's office that 'Sidi Mahomet, Emperor of Morocco, died suddenly last Sunday of an apoplexy while on horseback...'. P.R.O., FO 52/8.

92. The historian El Mansour refers to the instability which followed the death of Sidi Muhammad. El Mansour, *Morocco*, p. 88.

93. Mawlay al-Yazid, a son of Sidi Muhammad, succeeded to the throne based on the support of a number of powerful interest groups. *Ibid.*, 88-9.

94. In a letter of 9th August 1790, Irving informed his wife that 'I and my crew have at last obtained our final discharge from this country...' (Letter 32).

95. John Hutchison played a vital role in securing their release. Unfortunately, no personal papers or further official correspondence are available.

96. On his return to England on 26th October 1790, he again refers to 'our poor and dependent condition...' (Letter 34).

97. *Lloyd's List* of Friday 17th December 1790 records that the *Charlotte* in the command of Captain Davis had arrived at the Downs from Mogodore.

98. *Lloyd's List* of Friday 14th January 1791 records that the *Trial* in the command of Captain Baldry had arrived at Stangate Creek, London from Mogodore.

99. *Lloyd's List* of Tuesday 9th November 1790 (no. 244) records that the *Bacchus*, Prouting had arrived at Stangate Creek, London from Mogodore.

100. Irving wrote to his wife from Dartmouth on 26th October 1790 (Letter 34).

SECTION III: The Letters

Letter 1: 19th May, 1786. James Irving to his wife, Mary Irving, at home in Liverpool.

My dear lassy,

I have just found time to withdraw from the bustle a few minutes to address myself to you. The wind is at present rather contrary which oblidges us to keep the pilot a little longer, otherwise I should have said no more, but everything in nature has its use so has the foul wind in giving me this sweet opportunity to tell you that never till now did I know your worth. Oh! for a volley of these endearing embraces that I have so often received, I could at this moment almost smother you with caresses. I feel as if I was dismembered or deficient of a part essential to my existence. My sweet [?]lassy show no person this letter, it is not fit to be seen but it is at the same time the [deleted] feelings of a heart solely and enthusiastically yours. May God Almighty out of his inexhaustable benificence support and provide for you and the friends I have obtained through you, till I am enabled by his blessing to see you again in the cordial wish of him who lives only for you.

10 o'clock
May the 19th   J.I.

My compliments to all the gentlemen particularly Amoss, Mr. Hippins's family[1] etc. etc.

Letter 2: 13th August, 1786. James Irving on the west coast of Africa to Mary Irving.

New Callabar 13th August, 1786.

My dearest Mary,

The ship *Ally.* Dodson[2] f[...] this place sails tomorrow, and I most chearfully embrace the opportunity of informing you that I retain (through the assistance and protection of Divine Providence) my wonted health and contentment. The *Princess Venus* from Liverpool arrived here a week ago, and I had the mortification to find that you had neglected the opportunity. I readily excused you when I heard that the _Vulture_ sailed the same day but had called at Lisbon.[3] She is not yet arrived but when she does I flatter myself that what she will bring me will sufficiently compensate for my disappointment, but still my girl you should not have neglected or overlooked any opportunity. You see I don't as this is the third since my arrival, which is only a month.[4] In my last I hinted that our stay would be short, but I'm now sorry to say that most probably we shall be here two months hence. Trade is dull and [...] an exorbitant price. I expect (God willing) to be in the West Indies by the latter end of November or early in December. The above intelligence you may communicate to any person concerned or acquainted with our employers, as the captain's letter may miscarry and the least intelligence of the ship will be very satisfactory. I'm all impatience for the arrival of the _Vulture_ and _Golden Age_,[5] as you certainly have put two or three sweet billets on board each of them. You cannot be a stranger to the comfort and pleasure they will afford to an affectionate husband, who is toiling away with the sweat on his brow in a pestiferous climate under a vertical sun. Therefore, oblidge and please me at all times and in all places by your constant correspondence. In so doing you contribute much to the felicity of

> My dearest Mary,
> Your most loving husband,
> Jas. Irving

P.S. My duty and love to Granny and Mammy. I most sincerely wish them health and a comfortable enjoyment of the things of this life. The song book's lost. My dear and only brother George is most affectionately remembered,[6] also Cousin [...] and Longfield. I am making the necessary use of Spangenburgh's [...]. We are all alive that left Liverpool and in health, one excepted who is dangerously ill.[7]   J. I.

My best respects await the gentlemen lodgers and [...] friends Messrs. Hippins, Laycock and Jameson and their familys. I wrote Mr. Jameson per the sloop _Princess_ which he must have received by this time. In it I begged he would inform me of the prices of certain articles.

15th August, 1786.

My dearest girl,

The ship should have sailed yesterday but did not. I therefore subscribe this little note. I found it in some book or other and it seems to me so instructive that I have sent it for your perusal. I call it the art of happiness: "A good temper is one of the principal ingredients of happiness. This it may be said is ye work of Nature and must be born with us and so in a good measure it is, yet sometimes it may be acquired by art, and always improved by culture. Almost every object

A letter from James Irving to Mary Irving, 22nd November 1786.

that attracts our notice has its bright and its dark sides. He that habituates himself to look at the displeasing side will sour his disposition and consequently impair his happiness, while he who constantly beholds it on the bright side insensibly meliorates his own happiness and the happiness [...] about him". The above lines are so consistent with truth that I think I never saw anything [?]more so.

How does all friends in the north. [...] I think no opportunity will offer this 2 months for writing, therefore you must be as patient as possible.

>Farewell again,
>J. I.

15th August
I received your two by W. Amoss about ten minutes ago.

Letter 3: 22nd November 1786. James Irving, Barbados, to Mary Irving.

My dearest Mary,

With extatic pleasure am I again enabled to address you from a Christian country. I arrived off this place this morning after a passage of 46 days. A boat hath just come off with the letters, so that we proceed directly for Tobago where we expect to sell our cargo. God Almighty bless you my dear girl for your kind letter. I also received George's. I am [?]hurried beyond measure. Pardon my brevity, as I shall write on my arrival. God protect you, my compliments to everyone.

>Adieu,
>Jas. Irving

Captain Fargerer and fellow officers are all well.[8] Again adieu.
Carlisle Bay, Barbadoes. 22nd November, 1786.
We have been all healthy and buried 48 slaves.

Letter 4: 2nd December, 1786. James Irving in Tobago to Mary Irving.

>Scarborough Road in Tobago, 2nd December, 1786.

My dearest Mary,

My last voyage was from Barbadoes, where we staid about 2 hours, and proceeded to this place where we are safe moored. We have been here since the 25 ultimo and have not yet disposed of any of our very disagreeable cargo, but expect it on the 7th instant when our sale opens. Nevertheless I'm pretty certain of eating my Christmas dinner here (if able to eat one). I joyfully received your long wished for letter at Barbadoes inclosed in one from our very worthy friend Hippins with the prices of sundries annexed, in consideration of which make my most gratefull acknowledgements. Often, very often have I perused my dear girl's letter and each time with redoubled pleasure. In fine, I'm really and truly happy in the anticipation of joys that I fancy await me on again meeting with my dear little girl. O! that the omnipotent bestower of all good may preserve you from the numerous evils that so easily beset us and which from our vicious natures we are daily and hourly liable to, that he may keep you to bless the arms of an affectionate husband as an ample reward for the pangs of a long absence. Many thanks to you Mary for the various news your billet conveyed. Wish our cousin, Longfield, extreme joy in my name. It pleaseth me much to hear our uncle has so agreeably deceived you. Pride my girl generally takes its residence in little minds. I like the character or picture you have drawn of him, and we'll endeavour to fulfill your promise made to him if kind Providence deigns to escort me to my native shores. If he's enlisted under His [...] banner, may he long be happy and conspicuous in that corps and when the grisly visage of old age shall beset him may his children's children bear him off the field with eclat.

I'm nearly wearied of this unnatural accursed trade and think (if no change of station takes place) when convenience suits of adopting some other mode of life, although I'm fully sensible and aware of the difficultys attending any new undertaking, yet I will at least look around me.

As this is a French island I shall not have it in my power to purchase any produce of any kind, therefore shall bring the returns of my voyage home in my pocket. Brother George wants a [?]parrot. I'm sorry to say there is not one in ye ship, but if one can be procured here it shall be sent as directed as I have little reason to hope for a sight of him till he hath made his second voyage. Poor fellow, does he still like the Naval Department? [several words deleted]. I think I'll desist as our black cattle are intolerably noisy and I'm almost melted in the midst of five or six hundred of them.[9] There is a schooner bound for Barbadoes tomorrow morning early, and by he[...] [...] to transmit this to be forwarded from the [...]. God grant it may catch you as healthy as [...]ves.

Your most affectionate husband,
James Irvingg

Dear Mary,

The old folks are dutifully remembered. My compliments to every enquiring friend. Write to Langholm and satisfy the longings of good indulgent parents.[10] Have at you, on the first of March (God willing).

Letter 5: 3rd June 1787. James Irving, Africa, to Mary Irving in Liverpool.

Bonney River June 3rd, 1787.

My dearest girl,

Another conveyance per the brigg *Young Hero* occurs, and well I dare say its contents will be received. I was happy in getting opportunitys from Bassa and Anamaboe[11] to write you my good lass accounts of my health and happiness, the latter of which will be still heightened when I receive your vivifying epistles by the different ships. Many, many are the hours that I have spent most pleasingly on a retrospect of our loves. I dare say ~~your~~ our cogitations were reciprocal. I arrived ~~here~~ 29th May and found the *Garland* and a French ship here, the former with about 280 slaves the principal part of which she has put on board the brigg that arrived the day after us, with which she proceeds to the West Indies. While our ship lay without the barr[12] waiting for the spring tides, Captain Sherwood, Mr. Baker's nephew[13] and I went in our boat on board of Captain Forbes' and spent the principal part of two days.[14] He is perfect health and <u>has behaved with very great affability. He even gave me a bed and slept without himself. I most sincerely wish for his fortunate voyage.</u> He has been about a month in the river and expects to sail in 6 weeks. His officers and people are all pretty healthy [deleted]. We broke trade yesterday, and believe from what we can learn that our stay will be about 9 or 10 weeks. The space is not very long and if kind Providence deigns to keep us healthy, the time will slide away insensibly. As for you, you enjoy the sweet summer of your native country and I hope very happily. Would dare to hope that we shall warm our shins together over a clear fire when the hoary head of winter reigns crowned with a wreath of snow and boreas serenades us in every chimney. The *Garland* will be the next ship that sails and by her you may expect to hear from me. Captain Sherwood, Mr. Linton, McLeish and every other officer and man are in perfect health.[15] That the Almighty Creator and preserver of our beings and existence may keep you my dear [?]til in the same list is the hourly prayer of,

My dearest girl,

Your most affectionate and faithful husband

James Irving

P.S. Our mother and the old lady are most affectionately and dutifully remembered. My only brother George also possesseth my best and truest love. Our friends, Hippins, Laycock, Jamieson and others are also frequently thought of. McLeish desires his compliments, including Mrs. Robinson and Mrs. Tunstall.

How does Shirlock. Adieu.

J.I.

Letter 6: 20th October 1787. James Irving, Cuba, to his wife Mary Irving in Liverpool.

Havana 20 October 1787

Dear Mary,

I wrote your per a Londoner 5 days ago, but as Captain ~~Forbes~~ (the bearer of this) is immediately for Liverpool, in all probability this will be the first received. It leaves me healthy and tolerable fat. The Spanish beef and cabbage have wonderfull effects on an exhausted sailor after the long [...] African voyage. This is [...] a very plentifull [...] affording the necessarys [...] of live in great [...] and ~~the~~ we have them [...] without limitation. We expect to leave this [...] on the 1st November, God wil[...] [...] in consequence you may [...] expect us by Christm[...] [...]. I hope we shall toast [...] our shins together [...] Darby and Jo[...] over a clear coal fire and talk over the occurrences and incidents of our lives during our separation with a pleasing retrospect. I hav~~eing~~ nothing to say in this of the nature of news, should I say that the Havana is a city with walls, gates and barrs and most strongly fortified, almost impregnable. 30 sail of the line and 30,000 men would not be able to force a surrender. Each dwelling house is a citadel built of huge stones with its bastions and breastworks. In fine, its the strongest place I ever saw.

Adieu, I think I shall chase this very hard, if the dollars don't detain us. How that will be I cannot say but hope their treasury will receive a fresh supply before we are ready, if so await me.

>Dear Mary,
>Yours only,
>Jas. Irving

P.S. I hope our good mother and grandmother weather all their misfortunes with chearfullness and fortitude. My sincere love and duty to them and brother George, who I most sincerely hope to catch at home.

>Adieu   J. Irving

I'm sorry to say Captain Forbes has been unfortunate in respect of [...] [...] and [?]mercifully, he arrived here [...] days ago from Carriccas in good health and [...] to sail about the same time we do. [...] ship will make a pretty good voyage, you see [...] I'm poor luck, or rather Providence doth not forsake [...] that respects. What great reason have we to [...] [...]ankfull for such numberless ~~benefits~~ unmerited [...]its. Captain Sherwood and all our officers are well. We have buried 6 white people.

>Farewell again.

October 21 – I've been well all night, how have you spent it <u>lassy</u>? I sincerely hope most comfortably. The weather with you is grown cold and I imagine warm sheets are agreeable. How different from this torrid clime where universal heat is diffused in every void space and you cannot inspire without danger of being choaked by flies. Adieu with compliments to those you know your friends. [...] is vicious, never mind commonplace ones.

No opportunity to send this. 24th October 1787 and we expect to sail in the *Princess Royal* on the 4 November promiss.

J I

Letter 7: not dated [probably Spring 1788]. James Irving, on board the *Princess Royal*, to Mary Irving.

[the top half of the letter is missing]

... if it stands and keeps moderate [...] down channel. The ship proves very well so that you have nothing to fear from her late misfortune. If I should write you from Bonney desiring you'll make insurance, Mr. Hippins will with his usual friendship get it done for you. Remember me m[...] affectionately to him and family. Let me [...] beg that you'll behave with fortitude [...] that by the assistance of Divine Providence [...] be home in 9 months more or less, it is but [...] voyage. Cherish yourself with that reflection and [...] writing to me very often videlicet per ships *Elizabe[...]*, *Vulture, Ann, Hannah* or any vessel that sails [...] months after us to Bonney or New Callabar. Mrs. Sherwood will give you other information on that score. As Mr. Catteral has not time to write, therefore he desire ~~me to~~ his compliments and begs you would take the trouble of going to his house and tell Mrs. Cattaral what has happened and of his being very well. Cousin James desires his complimen[...]. I have wrote to my father informing him of me.[16]

[reverse side]

... remember me most [...] [...] [...] to our parents and brother and sisters. Heaven bless you is the present and will be the future prayer.

> My most beloved girl,
> Your affectionate husband,
> J. Irving

[...]closed is a letter I write that night I was [...] on board from you. Excuse everything you may find in it, as I thought it my duty to let you see it. Again farewell. Mind letters.

Letter 8: not dated [probably April/May 1788]. James Irving's younger cousin and namesake (James Irving II) to his parents in Langholm, Scotland.

On board the *Princess Royal,* clear of the banks.

Honoured parents,

I received yours in good time and was happy to hear that you were all well, as I and my friends are at present. We would have sailed long before this but as the ship [deleted] was going out of the dock into the river on the 23rd of last month, it being past high water and no wind, the strength of the tide turned her round and ran her aground and left her there till next tide. And she being so sharp bottomed lay on one side, which so strained her that she was all bent and leaked very much and she has been in the river ever since. But now she is straight and leaks so little that there is scarce enough to wash the decks and in the course of a month we expect there will be none. But, however, if it should continue it can do us no harm. And we have wated ever since she came out of the dock for a fair wind. But now the wind is fair and we are to sail the first tide. And I wrote this letter to send back with the pilot who leaves us after we are past the norwest boy. I have been abord 4 days and I eat in the cabin, and I have got a good coat bed and blankets and twilt[17] and I sleep very well. The other mate is a very good man, and I like my place very well. The captain gave me the coat frame and my couzen got me the blankets, twilt, jackets, trowsers, tea and sugar and everything that was necessary and I have everything as good as any on the ship. I forgot to write in my last about John Geddes's things as his mother told me to tell my couzin to lift the remainder of his money and pay Mrs. Tunstall,[18] but my couzin told his merchants are disaggreed and they would not give him the money without a receipt from John Giddes. Mrs. Lawson got a letter from her husband from the West Indies about 2 weeks ago. I have no news to write you but must conclude as the ship is under way with remaining,

Honoured parents,
Your dutyful son,
James Irving.

Give my love to my brothers[19] and compliments to enquiring friends.
J. Irving

Letter 9: 3rd May 1789. James Irving on board the *Anna* to his wife Mary in Liverpool.

Anna May 3rd, 1789.

My dearest girl,

You see I've been very smart out so far already with a fine promising wind. I expect to be round the Head early in the afternoon. Would fair hope you went to bed and got a comfortable sleep to quiet your agitated mind. Don't fret and distress yourself without cause. Providence if you confide in him is able and willing to support you in every situation in life. Think on these little matters and the reflection will afford balm to your mind. Go to church now and then or as often as you please. Take plenty of exercise in the open air, that is a practice that must be followed if you hope to be healthy. As the wind is so exceeding favourable the vessel runs out very fast so that I really cannot find time to say what I have within, but do rest satisfied my sweet girl the next I write shall be a very long one. Duty to all our good folks and again farewell. May God of his infinite mercy bless and protect you is, and shall be, the fervent prayer.

My dearest girl,
Your most loving and tender,
husband,
J. Irving

Letter 10: 24th June 1789. Captain Irving at 'Telling' in Barbary to John Hutchison, Vice-Consul at Mogodore [Essaouira] in Morocco.

Copy of the following letters received from Captain Irving.

Teilin June 24th, 1789.

Sir,

The subscriber a most distrest and suffering object takes the liberty to inform you that he had the most greiveous misfortune to lose his vessell on the Arab Coast opposite the west end of Forte Ventura on the 26th May ultimo. He and his crew, eleven in number inclusive, have been since that time in the hands of Arabs and Moors in a condition miserable beyond conception. A gleam of hope now ariseth from this indulgence writing to you. For the sake of Almighty God, neglect us not. We are Englishmen, and we hope good and loyal ones. Let that spirit of humanity which at present manifests itself throughout the realm actuate you to rescue us speedily from the most intollerable slavery. Suffer us not any longer like some poor Frenchmen about 10 or 12 miles from hence to be the slaves of Negroes, which reflects an unpardonate negligence on the man who should see them liberated. If we are allowed to stay here to toil and be maltreated under a vertical sun we shall soon be lost forever to ourselves, our wives and familys, our country and all we hold dear. My mate, surgeon and six men are with the Muley Abdrahman, at Gulimeme,[20] working while the sun shines in the open field. My second mate and an apprentice are somewhere else in the country. As I passed from Gulimeme hitherward, just got leave to speak to the Frenchmen. They tell me that they were informed one hundred dollars each was the sum demanded for their ransom. If that be so, most worthy Sir, advance it for us, and if required satisfactory security shall be given you for the sum. Our merchants are very affluent and some of us have friends that would be happy in having an opportunity to prove themselves such. I have two uncles in London, Mr. Joseph Smith and Captain Anthony Robinson on the East India Company half pay list, Castle Street, Long Acre. In fine, if the sum be so trifling it shall be sent to you with any interest required, and the favour deemed an unpayable one. Our vessel was the *Anna*, James Irving, master, off and from Liverpool, bound to the Gold Coast of Africa, her cargo, India, Manchester and hardware goods with about 20 tons salt, which was washed out. She had also 1000 dollars on board, all of which fell into the hands of the Arabs. When I set out was told that they were going directly to you, but I find shall be detained here till your answer determine our fate. The pass, commonly called the Mediteranean Pass is safe, number 7469.[21] I am almost naked having been plundered by the captors of everything. The people who at present claim me are pretty civil. Sheak Braham is my master, and he boards me with a Jew merchant named Aaron Debauny[22] My unfortunate shipmates know not what is become of me. Here follows a list of the crew:

James Irving, master
John Clegg, 1st mate
M. Francis Dawson, 2nd ditto a nephew of the merchants
James Irving, surgeon, a cousin of the master's.
Joseph Pearson – seaman
William Brown – ditto
John Richards ditto
Silvin Buckle ⎤
James Drachen ⎬ Portuguese blacks
Jack Peters ⎦
Samuel Beeley – apprentice

The vessell was owned by John Dawson Esquire of Liverpool. I cannot help again requesting your exertions in our behalf. Ample restitution shall be made you. O I hope you can feel for us, first suffering shipwreck, then seized on by a party of Arabs with outstretched arms and knives ready to stab us, next stripped to the skin suffering a thousand deaths daily, insulted, spit upon, exposed to the sun and night dews alternally, then travelled through parched deserts wherein was no water for 9 days, afterwards torn from one another and your poor petitioner marched to this place half dead with fatigue, whose only hope is in God and you. If you will condescend to answer this, satisfying me with respect to future expectations and whether we are or are not to be slaves, you'll confer an obligation that shall never be forgotten by your poor petitioner and most obedient servant.

James Irving Master

If any vessels are sailing for any Christian country, be pleased to communicate our fate. If my cousin who is with the Muley Abdrahman was conveyed hither, should then endeavour to make myself a little happier. I was the cause of his coming to sea, and now he is torn from me to work from morning till night without cause. Pardon the freedom I've treated you with, and the shamefull scrawl done with a reed. I am this moment told that 500 dollars per man is the sum expected. If so, will only be security for myself and my cousin the surgeon, till I get to England when I expect to redeem them by subscription if Government does not. I hope you'll not hesitate and doubt my security, as you may suppose what I've said is dictated by an honest heart and character that is well known as corresponding therewith. I am obliged to say so much as I've no opportunity otherwise to prove it. If ever I have through your [?]aid, I trust what I've said will be verifyed. J.I. If we are not to be directly set at liberty, be so kind as to obtain leave for me to come to Severa[23] to treat with you on the business.

Letter 11: 25th June 1789. Captain Irving in Barbary to either John Hutchison, Vice-Consul at Mogodore, or James M. Matra, Consul-General at Tangier. This is a copy of Irving's letter in Hutchison's handwriting, which is contained amongst Matra's correspondence.

Teilin 25th June 1789

Sir,

When I wrote the 2 half sheets inclosing this I was informed that Mr. Hutchison was Consul, but since that time have been made to know that he is at Fez on business and as the carriage of the letter won't leave this place these 2 days have again taken up my pen to address you, praying your assistance speedily. Let what I've said above be addressed to you, and let what I have farther to say stand as appending. I shall here give you the names of different persons who will be my vouchers in this melancholy business videlicet:

Captain Anthony Robinson, London.
William Sherwood , Liverpool.[24]
John Dawson Esquire – ditto.

Mr. Joseph Smith, London, or Mrs. Irving Number 2 Pownel Square,[25] Liverpool in my absence. If my own draught for whatever sum you expend on account of my cousin the surgeon, the second mate, Matthew Dawson and myself seems to you insufficient, any or all of the above gentlemen will pay it on demand. As for my chief mate and the rest of my poor people, it would be dishonest in me to say I will redeem them as I have not the sum, but if your goodness extends itself towards them, the whites particularly, I am almost certain restitution will be quickly made. The people here tell me if you do not pay for me or get me released, in ten days I go out to the fields to work at the corn. This you'll acknowledge to be hard. I was bred a surgeon originally, and God knows how I shall endure it. We are not on hostile terms with the Moors, and I have a pass granted by the Lords Commissioners of the Admiralty, therefore why are we detained my good Sir? Do what you can for us. Send me a note relative to the nature of our state, pray, send it by a safe conveyance. It will be thankfully acknowledged by yours etc.

Letter 12: 10th July 1789. John Hutchison, Vice-Consul, to James Irving at 'Telling' in Barbary.

Mogodore 10th July, 1789.

Captain James Irving

Sir,

I have received your letter of the 1st July. I hope mine of the 7th has got safe to you. Your sollicitude for your release and liberty is natural. I only wish my power was equal to my desires to procure them. I promise you, you should not remain a momment, but my last letter will have instructed you that no money I could offer, and would chearfully advance, can effect the purpose without the intervention of the Emperor, who will be very soon informed concerning you. The Prince Muley Absolem is now here.[26] I had immediate information conveyed to him of your situation and that of your people, and he immediately dispatched some horsemen to procure yours and their delivrance. I hope it will be soon effected. I am exceedingly sorry for your bad treatment. I hope it will be otherwise when Sheik Brahim receives my letter. I have again wrote him upon the subject. You seem to be very apprehensive of your cousin's being sent to the Emperor. Nothing could be more favourable to him, and I heartily wish you were all there now. You would have nothing to fear, and would presently be at liberty. The Emperor is at Morocco, and not at Fez as you have been informed. Be of good cheer and keep up your spirits. Be assured that I feel for you, as for a fellow subject under misfortune, which I will do everything in my power to alleviate. I am very truely

Sir,

Your most obedient humble servant,
John Hutchison and Consul

Letter 13: 21st July 1789. James M. Matra, Consul-General at Tangier, to William Wyndham Grenville at the Secretary of State's office in London.

Tangiers 21 July 1789

No. 12

Sir,

I have the honour to inform you that I have just received advice of the loss of the schooner *Anna*, James Irving, master, belonging to Liverpool, who on the 26 of last May was wrecked on the Arab Coast, opposite the west end of Fuertaventura. The crew consisting of eleven people were saved, two yet remain with the wild Arabs. The master, mate, surgeon and six men are about four days from Mogodore in the hands of Muly Abderhaman, an excommunicated son of the Emperor (his second) who remains independant of his father, and is maintained by the free Arabs.

The Prince I hear has promised to release them, and I hope he will. Meanwhile I have given orders to supply them, by means of the trading Moors, with what necessaries they want, and shall make application to Court that they may be released as soon as possible, but I have some doubts of immediate success. The Prince will listen to no terms from his father on any occasion, and I am afraid that the Emperor will not readily consent to let anybody treat with his son. The latter has made frequent application to the Commerce for wine and brandy, which in consequence of the Emperor's threats they were obliged to refuse, and probably now he will not part with the Christians, till he be well paid with the articles he wants, the supplying him with which in the state he is in with his father will be attended with great difficulty.

In my application to the Court, I shall strive to obtain leave to purchase them myself. At this time there are eight French seamen in the hands of the Arabs, who will not sell them to the Emperor, and he has refused to let anybody else buy them. While I am writing this, I have received an express by which I learn that Muly Islemmed full brother to Jezid,[27] and who he thereto has not been in favour, is just appointed to the command of all the south, in room of the favourite Abdslem, who being totally blind is to return to Court. It will be in that Prince's power to assist me, and as I am certain he will, I shall write to him.

When my express came away, the Emperor had not written to Jezid.

My friends inform me that as there was no vessel at Mogodore of sufficient accommodations for [?]finish, the Emperor means to write me for a frigate.

I have the honour to be with the greatest respect
>Sir,
>Your most obedient humble servant,
>James M. Matra.

Letter 14: 21st July 1789. John Hutchison, Vice-Consul, to James Irving at 'Telling' in Barbary.

Mogodore [?]21st July, 1789.

Captain James Irving

Sir,

I received a few days ago your letter of the 13th, and am happy to see that my last letter brought you some consolations, and that your health and spirits are in some measure restored. It will give me the utmost pleasure to contribute to your ease and comfort whilst under restraint, and to your deliverance as soon as possible. I can assure you that I am taking every step that may conduce to that end, and will continue my endeavours till it is accomplished. You will therefore, I hope, keep up your spirits and by frequent communication with your people, endeavour to make them easy. I observe the severall triffling things you have taken of the Jew[28] who will continue to supply you with whatever you may think necessary for yourself and people. I am glad to see that you have lately met with a little better treatment. I have received a letter from Sheak Brahim, wherein he promises to behave well to you and to use his endeavours in behalf of the rest of your people. To secure his good offices, I have sent him a cloth cloak he desired me to send him. It goes by this occasion, by which I have also sent 40 cubits of Oznaburg linnen which the Jew will get made up as you may direct him. Mr. Wynne also sends you a few triffles, and you may be assured that every necessary should be sent you were it not that any superfluity would be either stole or taken from you, or that any superior appearance would only tend to augment the difficulties of your redemption.

I have received the pass safe, and it shall be transmitted to the Admiralty Office in order that the bond for it may be cancelled.[29] I will take care in due time to furnish you with my official receipt for it. I have wrote sometime ago to your owner, Mr. Dawson of Liverpool, to acquaint him of your misfortune. That however need not prevent your writing yourself, as a few lines in your own handwriting must give satisfaction to your friends and relatives. I hope you will soon have the pleasure of seeing them. I earnestly wish it and am very truely

>Sir,
>Your most obedient humble servant,
>John Hutchison.

You may be assured that as soon as I am at any certainty regarding your fate I will advise you. Write by every opportunity, it will amuse you. I think it would not be amiss you should write a letter to James M. Mattra Esquire, His Majesty's Consul General, setting forth your situation and craving his assistance and protection. It will at least bring you acquainted should you meet together. [...] already informed of all the circumstances of your case, and I expect his answer every hour.

Letter 15: 1st August 1789. James Irving to Mrs. Tunstall, his mother-in-law, Liverpool.

Telling in Barbary, August 1st, 1789.

Honoured Madam,

Start not, the *Anna* is lost, but thank God we are all saved. We were carried ashore by a current on the 27th May last on the coast of Barbary, opposite the Canaries Islands, and have been since that time amongst the natives in a poor condition although healthy. Had I taken your advice and gone to Langholm this would not have happened, but it's now too late, at that time I could not have relished it. Let us keep Pope's opinion on events, whatever is, is right.

Have inclosed a letter to my Mary. Banish all doubts and fears, be chearfull and prepare her for the reception of it.[30] Shall not in this give you the particulars of the unfortunate accident, they would fill a volume. We'll talk them over in a winter's night. Fret not my good mother at this accident which distresseth us most severely. We shall yet be as happy, nay much happier, than those who have only eat of the bread of prosperity. As physics for the bodys good designed, so afflictions are the physic of the mind. My duty to the old lady, our grandmother, and most sincere love to happy George. Heavens bless and protect you all. We shall yet be as comfortable as if nothing had happened. At present God's will be done. Farewell

Honoured mother,
Your unfortunate son,
J. Irving.

Need make no apology for the appearance of this. Necessarys for writing are ~~neces~~ scare in this country. Compliments to neighbours and all friends, particularly the London ones.

Letter 16: 1st August 1789. James Irving, 'Telling' in Barbary, to Mary Irving in Liverpool.

Telling in Barbary

My poor dearest girl,

As a dream all our hopes and prospects are vanished. The *Anna* is wrecked and everything lost, yet be reconciled to your fate, God's will be done. Although the misfortune distresseth us most grievieously, yet by it I've learned what I never could have acquired by advice, that to be happy is not be ambitious.

I hope to be at home soon when we'll talk over our toils and difficultys and be yet happy, notwithstanding our poverty. Would advise you my pet, if your condition admits of it, to go spend some time with my father, no one will be half so welcome. Write to him and inform him of what has happened and ask his assistance, he will chearfully give it.[31] I shall trouble you with the particulars of the misfortune, but will relate it to you at the fireside as soon as I get home which I hope will be soon. Happier are those who have no ambition but toil hedgers and ditchers, than those who explore foreign countrys for what too often eludes their grasp.

I have now formed a firm resolution that if I get home and through God's assistance make another voyage to retrieve what I've lost, that the [...] shall bring me up, if I live on bread and water.

James and all the crew are well. They stay about 30 miles from this place. My dearest Mary repine not but be chearfull, everything is for the best. I might have missed this shipwreck, gone to Benin and died there.[32] There is no prying into the designs of Providence, he sees farther than we can and orders all aright. My duty and love to all our good family, and while alive I am

My poor dearest girl,
Your most affectionate husband,
J. Irving.

N.B. Blessed be God brother George did not go.

Letter 17: 2nd August 1789. James Irving at 'Telling' in Barbary to Mr. Hutchison, Vice-Consul at Mogodore. This is a copy in Hutchison's handwriting, contained amongst Matra's correspondence.

Telling 2nd August, 1789.

Mr. Hutchison Esquire.   <u>Copy</u>

Sir,

I again address you to communicate what information I've received concerning my people. I received their theirs in answer to mine of the 13th two days ago, and am very sorry to say, they write in bad spirits.[33] Their master, Prince Muley Abdrachman, most certainly intends to free them from their distresses by being their murderer. They say that when they are struggling under their burdens and exerting their utmost strength to accomplish their tasks, that he beats them most unmercifully and stands by till his Negroes beat them with sticks. One of them has an abscess in his hand that has penetrated through amongst the sinnews on the back of it and the surgeon is sick, his ailment is not mentioned. Yet notwithstanding, the same duty is expected from them, they must work if they die under their load. They also say that they scarcely obtain provision enough to sustain life. They had saved by some means or other 7 or 8 dollars, and one day being impelled by hunger offered one for anything that was eatable. As soon as he was informed thereof he ordered them to be stripped and searched, he found and took them from them. They also write me that 2 of the 6 pairs of shoes that where sent them, he hath taken and put on the feet of his own Negroes while they go barefooted, an action that would degrade a peasant, nay a highwayman, yet he deems it meritorious as he laughed heartily at it. My master arrived here last night from Gulimeme where he hath been these 18 days past, and hath brought with him one of the blacks. He says that he hath also purchased 2 of the sailors from Muley Abdrakman, but hath left them behind. He desires me to inform you that the price of each is settled, in all amounting on the nine to 1200 dollars, videlicet for the 7 with Muley Abdrackman, 900 and for the black and I, 300 dollars. You best know what use to make of this information. I must tell you that my master positively declines any business whatever with the Emperor. He says, he only pays a trifling sum for Christians, and my master will be paid the sum he now asks and in European goods. How it will terminate heaven knows. In spite of my fortitude I'm most unhappy, the prospect darkens as the time lengthens. I fear the Emperor hath either forgot us, or does not intend to redeem us. May God of his infinite mercy send our redemption soon, or their will be fewer of us to redeem in all probability, and the same money must be payd for us as if we had all survived it. The state of quiet and serenity that I boasted of and thought had attained, is almost wore away and two packets arriving within these few days without any letter or good news, depressed me still more. Yet while I live I'll hope (knowing that your best endeavours, are and will be exerted in our favour) that some wellcome news will one or other of these days arrive. I had almost forgot to inform you that the 2nd mate and apprentice have been at Gulimeme, but were taken away again on the 13th ultimo, the people here still say to Morocco. When I sit down to write to you, could write a whole quire but as I have nothing to say further than convey my feelings and anxiety after an emancipation from my slaving shall therefore not tresspass on your goodness, but write to Mr. Wynne and communicate the principal causes of my great unhappiness. I am

> Sir,
>> Your much obliged and most obedient servant,
>> Signed J Irving.

P.S. My people wish very much to change their master and supposed that much was in your power. Poor fellows, I heartily wish they had not been mistaken. My master will not allow me to [?]close the letter till I inform you, that the Muley Abdrackman means to send them into the gum country if not redeemed soon.

Have inclosed some letters for Liverpool, in forwarding of which you'll much oblidge J.I. An account of the shipwreck you'll see in Mr. Dawson's or Captain Sherwood's letters, which after you have read do beg of you to seall and forward.

Letter 18: 13th August 1789. John Hutchison, Vice-Consul, to James Irving at 'Telling' in Barbary.

Mogodore 13th August, 1789.

Captain James Irving

Sir,

I return your courrier as expeditiously as possible to acknowledge the reception of yours of the 2nd. The contents very much affect me, both on your account and that of your people, who, I am sorry to see are so inhumanely treated. I do assure you that I have been doing everything in my power, and will continue my best endeavours for your deliverance. Mr. Mattra, the Consul General, is doing the same and I hope that in a short time I shall have the pleasure of seeing you here, where you may be assured that your situation shall be made as easy as possible, and I hope you will meet with very short detention. I am truely sorry for the bad treatment your people meet with from the Prince with whom they are. I make no observations on his behaviour, as they are but too obvious. You will see by his taking away the shoes from the poor people, how useless it would be to send any superfluities and that consideration will, I hope, reconcile you to the deprivation of many necessaries I could wish to send you. The Jew Aaron, I hope, still continues to supply you with everything you may want either for yourself or people. I have now to inform you of the steps that have been taken, and the success they have had with regard to your redemption. The Emperor being informed of your misfortune, gave immediate orders to a Jew (Sintop Ben Attar) to send and purchase you at any price. The Jew is willing, but has not the power. I have wrote him to offer him every assistance in my power, and that I will be answerable for any difference there may be betwixt the Emperor's allowance and your real ransom. I also now write to Sheak Brahim that I accept of the proposition he makes of 900 ducats for the people with Muley

Abderhaman and 300 ducatts for you and the other man who is with you, and that the money shall be paid as soon as you arrive here. I have wrote the Jew to be bound for the money and to accompany you here, or send a proper person with you. In short, if the twelve hundred ducats will relieve you and I have every reason to think it will, you have nothing farther to fear. Comfort yourself, and send comfort to your people. Your second mate and apprentice are arrived at Morocco.[34] They are well. The Emperor has given them up to his son, Muley Absolem, till the others arrive. I have wrote the Prince begging he would be so good as send them to me, and I hope to see them in a few days and in the meantime have given orders to supply them with necessaries. You will see by the above narrative, that I am doing everything in my power for you. I expect speedy and agreable effects. Keep up your spirits, comfort your people and believe me to be with sincerity

> Sir,
> Your most humble servant,
> John Hutchison.

Letter 19: [28th] August, 1789. John Hutchison, Vice-Consul, to James Irving at 'Telling' in Barbary.

Mogodore [...] [...]ugust, 1789.

Captain James Irving

Sir,

I have received your severall letters of the 12th, 17th and 22nd current, the first by the bearer, being the courrier you sent and I now return, who only delivered his letters the 26th. The last I received yesterday by one of the returned courriers. I am glad to see that your master was pleased with his cloak, and that you felt some good effects from it. I wish he may continue in the same mind till you are out of his power, which I have every reason to think will be soon. I shall forward your letter for Tangier by first occasion.[35] I see that your sensibility has taken an alarm from my suggesting to you the propriety of writing the Consul General. My suggestions did not proceed from any new difficulty that has, or can occur, but from my thinking it proper for every British subject in this country to apply for protection to the person who has His Majesty's Commission for that purpose. I am sorry to see that the few things sent you begin to attract the avidity of your tyrants and on that account, shall only continue my orders to Aaron, which you will make such use of as you please. I must beg leave to caution you not to make use of the term infidels, either in your letters or discourse when speaking of the Moors. They look upon the term as the most oprobrious in their language, and as they have the power in their hands, it may operate to your prejudice. You will excuse my caution. I see your master desires a little tea and sugar. I send it by the bearer who will deliver it to Aaron, and he to you or Sheak Brahim, as you choose. It is no great matter and will help to keep him quiet.

I am very glad to see that my letter of the 13th conveyed some comfort to you. You may be as[...] that I write you nothing, but what had been executed and what I firmly believed would have immediately taken place. There has intervened some small obstacle, which however will soon be obviated. When I wrote you and made the proposition to Sheak Braham it was, as you will see by my letter, in the intelligence that a Jew, Sintop Ben Attar,[36] was commissioned by the Emperor to purchase you. My interference was, consequently, under his supposed sanction. The Jew arrived here and informed me that it was true the Emperor had given him such orders, but had immediately withdrawn them and desired his son, Muley Absolem, to do it. I was consequently obliged to stop farther proceedings till I am authorised either by the Emperor or the Prince, who is now at Tarrudant. I have couriers absent to both on the business. I have made no scruple to inform you of the above circumstances, lest you should imagine something worse. Your captivity will, I hope, soon have amend. Mr. Dawson and the apprentice are with me, the Prince having sent them to me on his leaving Morocco. Mr. Dawson I am sure would write you, but I have given him permission to go on board ship for a day or two and he is not yet come on shore. I hope Sheak Brahim will be more reasonable than you seem to imagine, not that I believe he would be at all scrupulous about breaking his word if he could get anything by it. With regard to the Frenchmen, I do not think they are purchased yet. There came a Frenchman here a few days ago, who has been long in the country. He has been purchased here for [?]account of the Emperor for 110 dollars. I hope soon to send you better news, and am very truely

> Sir,
> Your most obedient humble servant,
> J[...] [...]tchison

Letter 20: 11th September 1789. John Hutchison, Vice-Consul, to Captain Irving at 'Telling' in Barbary.

Mogodore 11th September, 1789.

Captain James Irving

Sir,

Since my last of the 28th August, yours of the 23rd and 3rd September have come to hand. I pay due attention to their contents although it has not been in my power to answer them at large, nor will it now, on account of being very busy. I take due note of the double dealing and tergiversation of the people you are with. There is no remedy but patience, the exercise of which will not I hope be long necessary. As to Aaron, I know your character of him to be true. Indeed I believe there is not an honest Jew in the country. His conduct as well as that of Sheak Brahim is naturall enough, all for self interest, but we must make such use of them as we can. I have the pleasure to acquaint you that I received a most favourable answer to the letter I wrote [deleted] concerning you to the Prince Muley Absolem. He says I may make myself perfectly easy regarding the Christians, and that they shall be with me in 15 days. He immediately gave orders to an Alcaide Mohammed Dlimy to procure and send them immediately.[37] I have the greatest hopes that the orders will be executed, and wait with much impatience to see the result. Your master's views will also probably be answered as it is that same Alcaide, or a brother of his, who possest the Frenchmen, 4 of whom have been sent here and from hence to Morocco, I believe in order to be sent to their consul at Sallee. I am glad to see that some more of your people are with you. I do not apprehend anything of the Prince Muley Abderhaman's intention to send the people to the southward, or if he has, that his brother's application will prevent it. I can say no more on that head, except that if I have not any satisfactory news when the 15 days are expired, I will again recur to the Prince.

As to Aaron's claim about the 16 dollars, I think it by no means reasonable. It is however needless to enter any dispute about it at present, as the settling it must depend upon the final adjustment as well as the Sheak's claim about his horse. With regard to Aaron's insisting about boarding you, I am not very sorry he should do so, as you will be better treated and a triffle of expence more or less does not signify. I have formerly allowed people in your situation, so much per day in money to be paid into the captain's hands and to find themselves. Pray do you think you could venture to do so without a risk of the moneys being taken from you? I will give immediate orders as soon as you tell me what will be sufficient, but I hope we shall very soon have no occasion for it. I heartily sympathise with you and am sincerely

>Sir,
>Your most obedient humble servant,
>John Hutchison.

Letter 21: 27th September 1789. J.M. Matra, Consul-General, to Captain James Irving at 'Telling'.

Tangiers 27th September, 1789.

Sir,

I have [...] just received your letter of the 10 August.[38] The moment your unhappy situation was known, every effort was began for your relief and shall be continued till you are all released from the wretched state you are in.

I am happy to find Mr. Vice Consul Huchison has found means to convey you a few necessaries. He has directions to supply you with whatever can with safety be conveyed, and as I know his attention and humanity I am certain you will have much reason to be content with his exertions. I have authorised him to pay the sums demanded for your ransom whenever the Arabs are willing to accept of it, which I hope by this time is done as Prince Abslem has the Emperor's authority to undertake the business, and to induce the Prince to be active in your favour I have promised and now send an English doctor down the Arab country to attend to his health, a place that I certainly would not have risked a subject in were it not for the prospect of being useful to you and your people.[39]

I am in hopes that you will receive this letter in Mogodore, but if by any unexpected conduct in the Arabs your redemption should be delayed, do not lose your courage, for depend upon it no time will be lost, nor no expence spared to procure the liberty of you and your people.

I am,
Sir,
Your most obedient
humble servant,
James M. Matra.

Letter 22: 7th October 1789. James Irving, 'Telling' in Barbary, to Mary Irving in Liverpool.

Telling 7th October, 1789.

My dearest girl,

I wrote you sometime ago, which I hope you have received, giving you a short account of my misfortune and my expectation of being soon at home. I have however been detained by one cause and another, and Mr. Hutchison our good Vice-Consul and Mr. Atkinson Wynne, another gentleman at Mogodore, both of them assure me by letter that we shall all very soon be at liberty to return home. Mr. Wynne hath been exceeding kind in sending me different things. Keep up your spirits, my good pet. I am in health and you may most assuredly expect me soon. Kisses, duty and love to our good friends singly and collectively. It will answer no purpose to enter into a detail of every occurrence since the shipwreck as they would fill many sheets. I am

> My dearest wife,
>> Yours affectionately till death,
>>> J. Irving

P.S. Brother George is I dare say returned from his voyage and sailed again. If you should write to him remember me most affectionately, as also to our friends in the north and south. I shall in all probability come to London, but do not mean to show myself as my condition will not be very pleasing to myself particularly. I shall write you the instant I get my feet on my native shore.

Letter 23: 1st November 1789. John Hutchison, Vice-Consul, to Captain Irving at 'Telling' in Barbary.

Mogodore 1st November, 1789

Captain James Irving

Sir,

I had the pleasure of writing you the 15th and on the 17th. I received yours of the 7th which had no opportunity of answering till now. I am glad you received the medecines and that your fever has in a manner left you. I hope the other symptoms will have gradually disappeared.[40] It also gives me pleasure to hear that Aaron has a little mended his behaviour. I hope you are by this time, or will be very soon, out of his power as I have repeated letters from the Prince that I might fully depend upon your being all redeemed and immediately sent up to Morocco. I find he has been as good as his word with regard to your cousin and three of the people who were with you.[41] I had a letter from Mr. Irving the 27th from Tarudant. They have received some little necessaries from a Frenchman at that place by my directions, and were to set out next day for Morocco where they are no doubt arrived. Mr. Clegg and the two others[42] arrived there the 3rd. Every care shall be taken of them, for though they are not immediately under my eye, they are in a situation much preferable to their former one, and where I can immediately render them every necessary assistance. I hope your being left behind the others will not have affected you. I do not comprehend the cause, but suppose it must be owing to Dlaimy's having no more money [?]than purchased the other 3. I have again wrote the Prince, and as the surgeon Mr. Lempriere from Gibraltar is now at Tarudant[43] there is no doubt but that you will immediately [deleted] join your people. I heartily wish it. Be of good cheer, your deliverance I hope is near.

I beg you will not make yourself uneasy about any expences I may have been at, that matter will be easily settled. I only wish to be of service to you. Your letter for Mrs. Irving was forwarded the 19th under Mr. Wynne's cover to the ladies of his family. I am sincerely

      Sir,
         Your most humble servant,
            John Hutchison

Letter 24: 9th November 1789. George Dalston Tunstall, to J.M. Matra.

Honoured Sir,

Please to consider this my humble and distressing petition, which not only concerns me for the welfare of a dear brother-in-law, but many others who have had their fond relations torn from them by being unfortunately wrecked upon that barbarous coast which, from all accounts, is so deserving of its title.

Reflect Sir, upon the distressed situation of a beloved brother and his fellow sufferers, as also of an unhappy only sister who labours under the greatest anxiety of mind for her dear husband's liberty. His name is James Irving, he was master of a small schooner called the *Anna* belonging to Mr. Dawson merchant in this town bound to the coast of Africa, but unfortunately getting into a strong current off the Isle of Furtaventura setting to the eastward was hurled on shore near Cape Non. This event happened on the 27th of May about 8 o'clock in the evening, they continued by her till morning when she went to pieces, they then left her taking with them some provisions with an intent to travel to Santa Crose but were next morning taken by the Arabs and by them conveyed back into the country.[44]

My distressed sister received a letter from her husband dated Telling the 1st of August wherein he mentions that his case for some time has been very deplorable, and that the rest of the crew, which I believe consists of 15, are distant from him near a day's journey.

Honoured Sir, your interest with the Emperor I have no doubt might be of infinite service in effecting their speedy release. Consider Sir, they are all British subjects, and demands from those barbarians liberty. By fulfilling this the humble petition of a young sailor (who will be ever ready and willing to serve my king and country upon all occasions, as my late father who died at Madrass in the year 71 soon after my birth had the honour of doing as lieutentant in the navy on board his Majesties Ship the *Orford*) you will make the wretched happy. I remain honoured Sir

      Your humble petitioner and one who
      will ever offer up his prayers for your
      safety, honour and welfare
      George Dalston Tunstall.

Letter 25: 11th January 1790. John Hutchison, Vice-Consul, to James Irving in the city of Morocco.

Mogodore 11th January, 1789.

Captain James Irving

Sir,

I received your favour of the 2nd with much satisfaction as I began to be apprehensive that my letter with the parcell had miscarried, though that could hardly be the case, as the man that carried them is well known to me and has his family here. It is certain that we have both suffered by miscarriage of letters, but that inconvenience is now, I hope, over as the conveyances are much more frequent and sure to and from Morocco than Tilling. Aaron I know is a rascall, so are they all and entirely attached to their own interest. I am well acquainted with their impositions, but there was no choice or doing without them, so that we must have patience. Your receipts for the disbursements at Tilling have not yet reached me, nor have I received your letter informing me of the conditions of your ransom. As to any future claim it can noways concern us, they must settle it with the Emperor to whom we are only (under God) to look for your ultimate delivrance from this country. I am very glad to see that the Prince was so considerate as to supply you with some necessary cloathing. The contents of the parcell will, I hope, have also been of some service and I now send you a cloth coat and waistcoat and a pair of black breeches, which were making when I received your letter. They are made after Mr. Wynne's measure, as I saw by your few lines to him that you were much of a size. The cloth is the same I had made up for your officers, I could find no better here. Mr. Matra is continually pursuing every measure that can lend to your delivrance. All our hopes at present center in what Mr. Lempriere may be able to effectuate by means of Muley Absolem. Should his endeavours fail, other means must be tried. Mr. Matra has sent home to Government a list of your names, and there is little doubt but that our Gracious Sovereign will write the Emperor to demand you, so that at any rate you will not, I hope, be long in captivity. I am glad your present situation is not disagreable to you, and that the necessary subsistence is not wanting. If it should, I must beg leave to tell you that it will be your own fault, as you will always find me ready and willing to supply whatever may be necessary for yourself or people. In the same parcell with your cloaths there is also 5 pair trowsers and 7 check shirts, which Mr. Clegg wrote me were necessary for the people. I would also have sent the 3 jackets but cannot get them ready for this occasion. As to hats, there are none to be procured here. If they can point out any succedaneum,[45] they shall be supplied. As to the money part of the supply, Mr. Clegg and your officers will have informed you that the Emperor allows every person an ounce a day each, which, for the bare subsistence, I thought sufficient, any other necessaries to be supplied by my order. To Mr. Irving, Clegg and Dawson I allow an ounce *per diem* extraordinary. Should you think any addition necessary to this arrangement, you will let me know. With regard to yourself, you will make your own regulations for your necessary subsistence. I have ordered the Jew who pays the others to supply you with what you may call for, and in case he should be absent and have left nobody in his place, the son of the man at whose house you are at, Joseph Ban Mushee Ben Behé, will supply you. Mr. Wynne has made a short trip to Portugal. Let me hear from you by every occasion, and believe me to be very sincerely

Sir,

Your most obedient humble servant,

John Hutchison

My compliments to Mr. Clegg, Mr. Irving and Mr. Dawson.

In the box with the things there are also 10 pairs old stockings and an old black handkerchief. Inclosed is a letter for Joseph Ben Behé from his father. He will supply you with whatever you may want in case the other should be out of the way.

Letter 26: 18th January 1790. John Hutchison, Vice-Consul, to James Irving at Morocco [Marrakech].

Mogodore 18th January, 1790.

Captain James Irving

Sir,

I received last Saturday afternoon your letter of the 10th by the Moor who carried you your small parcell. I hope the other Moor I sent with a box and my last letter of the 11th, will have delivered both safe long before now. I principally write this at the desire of the Jew who brought me your former letter, of whose departure however I was too late informed to be able to answer your letter at length. Indeed by what is reported here since yesterday, it would be needless, as it is reported that the Emperor intends immediately to send you all to this place and to put you under the care of one of our countrymen, a Mr. Layton (Milbank, as the Emperor calls him) a merchant here.[46] Since you are condemned to stay in the country for sometime longer I am glad you are to come here, as I hope you will find it on many accounts more agreable than at Morocco, and it will always give me much pleasure nothwithstanding the Emperor's putting you under the care of another, to render you every service in my power. Mr. [deleted] Lempriere's case is certainly extremely hard, but I hope it only proceeded from a misunderstanding and has been set to rights before now. If however he should be sent down with you, pray give my compliments to him and tell him I expect he will take up his lodgings with me, as the Emperor can have no right to treat him as a prisoner.[47] I am sorry for the trouble you had with those thievish Jews. They did not however venture to make any appeal to me on the business, nor did they ever inform the master of the house where you live about the matter, a sure sign of their guilt. My last will have directed you, in regard to any additional supply you may think necessary for yourself. My compliments to your officers. I am very truely

Sir,

Your most obedient humble servant,

John Hutchison.

Letter 27: 31st January 1790. James Irving at Mogodore to his wife Mary Irving.

Mogodore 31st January, 1790.

My dearest girl,

I wrote you from the city of Morrocco three weeks ago, which I hope on your account particularly is received.[48] I have now the pleasure to tell you that after many difficultys and inconcievable hardships every one of us are got safe here in perfect health and are under the care of our humane Consull Mr. Hutchison, who supplys us with cloaths and the necessarys of life, so that nothing is wanting but the Emperor's leave to visit our dearest connections and native country, which the Emperor himself told me he could not grant til our Gracious Sovereign shall write to him requesting it. This we daily expect as Mr. Matra, his Majesty's Consul General at Tangier, hath wrote a long time ago to the Secretary of State's office concerning us.[49] Be comforted therefore, my dear Mary, and bear up under your sufferings with the fortitude of a good Christian, and to encourage you let me assure you that I am no longer a slave ~~and~~ but enjoy my liberty in every respect (that of leaving the country excepted) and expect very soon to leave this country and to enjoy the smiles of fortune once more. She hath jilted me once, but you know she's fickle and may next time be propitious. Let us be virtuous and Providence will uphold, as whom he loveth he chastiseth and afflicteth in order to render them worthy of his future care. Be cheerfull and repine not, my conduct will bear any scrutiny however severe and we shall flourish the more after our pruning.

This is a most hospitable place. There are 7 Christian mercantile houses here, 3 of which are English and they seem to strive who to outdo each other in kindness and hospitality. My good friend Mr. Wynne is at present on a voyage to

Malaga, have therefore not seen him. He corresponded a long time with me during my stay in the Arab country at Telling and his and Mr. Hutchison's kind letters contributed very considerably to my life and support. I dare now tell you what before I thought proper to conceal that my life through sickness during my slavery had well nigh fallen a prey to it. Blessed be God I have fairly weathered all and enjoy good health and as good spirits as can be supposed after so severe a trial, the remembrance of which will never be erased. Mine once was the condition and this the country to give a person a proper relish for the happiness Englishmen enjoy, to cure the epicure and the spendthrift and instill into them true notions of oeconomy and frugality.

I have been most anxious to know your state and how you have withstood the storm of fate, but as I have every prospect of being soon with you I think it will be improper to write now. Mr. Hutchison informs me that he wrote to Mr. Dawson instructing him how to ge[...] [...] [...], but as Mr. Dawson had [...] [...] [...]pposed as it was very reason[...] [...] [...]uld not write, and perhaps you was not acquainted with the mode of conveying a letter. I shall therefore rest in hopes that Providence watcheth kindly over you, and every one of you collectively. My constant prayers have been offered up for you all. Assure our mother and grandmother of my most dutifull and affectionate remembrance of them as also of my dear brother and fellow tar, George, our parents in the north and every other relation and friend. My pet, forget not to relieve their anxietys by letter. Inform them of James's health and welfare, he is grown in stature most amazingly.[50] Farewell, may God Almighty take you into his care and keeping, is and shall be the constant prayer of

> My dearest girl,
> Your most affectionate husband,
> J. Irving.

P.S. in looking over some newspapers, I see that the officers of the East India Company are ordered abroad. How does Uncle Anthony [...] [...] it is a very trying one.

Letter 28: 25th March 1790. James Irving II to his parents in Langholm, Scotland.

Mogodore in Barbary 25 March, 1790.

Honoured parents,

I now again sit down to let you hear that your unfortunate son enjoys good health and all that he can wish except the liberty to return to our native country, but that blessing we expect very soon as Mr. Hutchison's (the English Consul) clark writes from Morroco, which is the place which the Emperor resides at present, that the Emperor has wrote to the Governor of Gibraltar for the loan of a frigate to go to Alexandria with one of his sones who is going a pilgrimage to Mecca which if the Governor will grant, and there is no doubt but he will, the Emperor will deliver all of us up to him and likewise allow the trade of fresh provisions (duty free) from Tangier to Gibraltar which has been stopt for some time past.[51] I, therefore, beg that you will give yourselves no concern about me as we are now in a town where there are Christian merchants and shipping of different nations, which are very kind to me and we live very well. Have a house to ourselves, got good cloaths and [?]alwise money in our pockets and nothing to do but amuse ourselves, so that we are just as well as we could wish only loosing our time. I need say no more at present, as I hope in a short time to be sitting at your fireside where I will tell you all that has happened to us since we came into Barbary. I need only say since we came here we have been very happy, with the thoughts in a short time of enjoying our long lost liberty and being again in our native country. I therefore bid you adew with wishing all that's good attend you.

Honoured parents,
I am,
your very dutiful son,
J. Irving

P.S. My couzen joins in his love to you and my brothers and other friends, J. Irving.

N.B. I write this by an English brig who sails in 2 days. My couzen writes to Mrs. Irving by the same vessel and desires her to write to Langholm.

Letter 29: 26th March 1790. James Irving at Mogodore to Mary Irving.

Mogodore 26th March, 1790.

My dearest girl,

An anxious care for your quiet and peace of mind induceth me to embrace every opportunity that offers to let you hear from me. In my last from this place, I ventured to inform you of my present and part of my past condition. I have still ye same liberty and indulgence, and although am still I continue the Emperor's property, yet have little reason to call myself a slave, but rather a prisoner at large, restrained only from going aboard any vessel or returning to my native country and to you my poor sharer in misfortune. I blame myself much for not instructing you in the method of getting a letter conveyed to me. Heaven only knows how anxious I am to hear from you. Ten long months have elapsed since the fatal shipwreck and not any letter from or account of you has reached me.

God forbid it should arise from any other cause than from your ignorance of the conveyance. Mr. Hutchison, our Vice Consul here, at my desire wrote Mr. Dawson communicating the disagreeable intelligence and put him in the method of writing to me should he have anything to say. I fear you were not informed thereof. Mr. Hesketh Esquire, our late mayor, will forward your letters for me should I be redeemed before any of them reacheth me. The loss will be immaterial, but if they find me here will contribute much to my felicity. Inform me how Mr. Dawson received the account of my misfortune with other particulars, as also whether Uncle Anthony goes or is gone to India.

A treaty is at present on foot between the Emperor and the Consul General respecting our release. How it will succeed or terminate I am uncertain, only I can assure you that sooner or later it must end in our final release. My dear girl, my heart breaks for your destitute situation. How you are supported I know not, neither do I know what advice to give. I have wrote to Captain Sherwood my good friend and requested his assistance, should you find it necessary. Your poor mother's resources must fail. I hope other friends forsake you not in the day of tribulation. God strengthen and support you all, despair not this is our day of trial. Providence will yet befriend us and restore me to you when I hope I shall be enabled to provide for you. The time I hope is not far distant when our present and past sufferings shall only be remembred for our benefit. We are all here and healthy except one of the blacks who I gave an account of in one of my former letters.[52] Providence hath most wonderfully preserved us through a dreadful series of hardships. He is able still to support us. Our distress is now only mental which we endeavour to lighten as much as possible by reading and other amusements.

Our grandmother, mother and brother George are most dutifully and affectionately remembred, as also our parents in Scotland. Write them concerning me and James. Assure them ~~I am~~ we are healthy and entertain strong hopes of being soon in my native country. Adieu for a while. Heavens bless and keep you is the daily prayer of

> My dearest wife,
> Your most affectionate but
> unfortunate husband,
> J. Irving

Mr. Wynne is not in this country at present. He went from here on a voyage to Malaga. I long to see him, to thank him for his attention to me when in slavery.

Direct me under cover to Messrs. Gwyn and Hutchison, Mogodore to the care of Mr. John Metcalfe, merchant, London, or to Mr. John Anthony Butler, merchant, Cadiz, or to Thomas Gavino Esquire, Gibraltar, or to Messrs. Isaac

Megueres and Co. ditto – Our Uncle Smith will put it into the hands of Mr. Metcalf [...] [...]ou have no reason to fear *its miscarri*[...]

Letter 30: 20th May 1790. Captain William Sherwood to unspecified individuals.

Liverpool the 2nd May, 1790.

Sir,

Not having the honour to be personaly acquainted with you, I must first beg your pardon for the liberty I take in addressing you. I next beg leave (with Mrs. Robinson, Mrs. Tunstall, Mrs. Irving) to crave the indulgence [...] [?]forwarding the inclosed copys of letters from [?]Mrs. I[...]. He had the misfortune to lose a fine new vessell on the coast of Barbary as he was perseuing his pass[...] out of this port towards the Gold Coast of Africa. [...] vessel belonged to Mr. John Dawson of this place, and although Mr. Irving has mett with this unfortunate accident I know him to be as carefull, sober and industrious a man as ever lived. I've had an opportunity of knowing him well, he haveing been two voyages with me to Africa.[53] If your interest can be of any service in relieving him from this present unhappy state and in restoreing him to his native country I [...] no doubt but you chearfully would do your [?]utmost endeavours for that purpose, for doing which you would be justly entitled to the gratefull thanks of him, his family and of, Sir, your much obliged and

Obedient humble servant
W. Sherwood

The inclosed letters Mrs. Irving and myself will thank you to forward to Mr. Metcafe as soon as possible and Mrs. Irving no doubt will be anxious to hear of their welfare.

[there is a note in a different hand appended on the letter as follows:

[...] from Captain Sherwood who is supposed to be one of the most respectable commanders in the African trade from the above port and in the employ of Messrs. Baker and Dawson.]

Letter 31: 8th June 1790. James Irving at Mogodore to Mary Irving.

Mogodore 8th June, 1790.

My dear girl,

I wrote you 5 days ago by a brigg belonging to Pulhely in Wales[54] and bound for London, the master of which showed us many civilitys while he lay in the harbour. In it I gave a loose to the sense of our situation, and the little attention showed us either by our friends or by our Court. Should I, in the heat of my chagrin from the sensibility of my heart have said anything to hurt your feelings, I flatter myself you will be very ready, my suffering partner to forgive me.

I have nothing to communicate to you of the nature of news, as my last explained my prospects and expectations. The Emperor is expected at <u>Morocco</u> in 20 days when he will be again solicited by Mr. Hutchison Esquire, His Brittannick Majjesty's Vice Consul here. I am under many obligations to that gentleman who hath used every means in his power to alleviate our afflictions, as hath also his ~~partner~~ commercial partner Mr. Gwyn. Mr. Wynne, who I mentioned in some of my letters as having corresponded with me and sent me some necessarys whilst I was in slavery at Telling, is not yet returned from Malaga but is daily expected as a war with Spain is rumoured about.

My dear Mary, it is a most melancholy truth that it is entirely out of my power to assist you in any respect. I can only pray for you, and trust to friends and a benevolent world for your support. O! the reflection is a cutting one, but the will of heaven be done. Had I the liberty of acting I doubt not but my endeavours are fully adequate to produce a tolerable support for us. That day through the help of Providence will yet come and all shall be well. I live on the hope of obtaining my release and receiving letters from England. I hope you have a dozen at least on their way hitherward.

My officers and people continue in health and are still with me.

Our good mother, grandmother, brother George are most affectionately remembred, as are also every relation and welwisher. Respectfull compliments to Captain Sherwood and family, Linton, Maxwell, [?]Amon etc. etc. etc. I have wrote to Scotland to the old folks there and shall continue to let you hear from me by every opportunity, while I am

> My dear girl,
> Your most affectionate
> and forlorn husband,
> J. Irving

Letter 32: 9th August 1790. James Irving at Mogodore to Mary Irving.

Mogodore 9th August, 1790.

Dearest wife,

I wrote you about a month ago and could not at that time give you any very flattering hopes of our being immediatly released. I can now with much satisfaction inform you that I and my crew have at last obtained our final discharge from this country, and expect to leave it in a month or 5 weeks in the brigg *Bacchus*, Captain Prouting, at present lying in this road and bound to London. I dare say my good girl you'll feel as happy as I do on the termination of my bondage, which I have weathered with ten thousand difficultys. Such a severe affliction happens seldom and one such trial in a man's life, is more than sufficient to prove his fortitude [deleted]. On my arrival in London, should it please God, I'll write immediatly as it will not be convenient for me to come directly for Liverpool for many reasons. 1st. my shabby appearance, 2nd. the loss of my certificate as a surgeon, which it will be necessary (let whatever may happen) to get renewed,[55] and 3rd. my uncertainty with respect to the state of you and family as also of Mr. Dawson's sentiments. But you may be assured on these difficultys being removed, I shall make the best of my way for Liverpool. We are all well. Love, duty and best respects to our parents, George and everyone who you have found friendly. Farewell, I am still

> Dearest wife,
> Yours most affectionately,
> J. Irving.

A list of James Irvings cloths:

> 1 coat, waistcoat and breeches
> 1 pair of black sattin breech
> 1 shirt
> 2 neck cloths
> 2 pocket handkerchiefs
> 1 pair of black silk stockings
> 2 Guinea cloths
> 2 pieces of nonkeen[56]
> 8 silllk handkerchiefs.

Letter 33: 22nd September 1790. Mr. Robson, Liverpool, to William Graham, a physician in Gibraltar.

Liverpool September 22nd, 1790.

My dear Doctor Graham,

I have this afternoon been solicited to write you by a vessel that sails for Gibraltar tomorrow. Had I known of the opportunity, would have wrote if it had been only to tell you of my welfare, which at all times I know you will be glad to hear of. The enclosed is a letter that I beg your utmost attention to get it forwarded through channel, so as poor Irving may receive it. It's on a case of humanity. I know you have a good heart and the feelings of a man, and will use your utmost endeavours to find an opportunity which never has been yet, that he may receive this. Hear now I'll tell thee. About the time we was taking the fresh air last summer in the Boarders and sporting among the rose buds on the banks of the Esk,[57] Jimmy Irving got the command of a schooner to go the coast of

Africa. Three weeks after he left Liverpool ran ashore in the night on the coast of Barbary. The natives siezed the vessel, himself and crew and marcht them into the interior parts of the country and made slaves of them. To recount the hardships they underwent would be too tedious and give no pleasure to the feelings of Willy Graham. Chance gave him an opportunity to write to the English Consul at Mogodore, who used his intrest so far with the grandee there as to get them made prisoners on parole at ~~Mogodore~~. Since Mr. Irving has been at Mogodore, Mrs. Irving has heard from him often and has as often wrote, as well as many more of his friends here but he never has received any of the letters though they have been sent from the Secretary of State's office to the Consul at Mogodore. In his last letter he wrote with an unusual gloom over his spirits, and thinks his friends now in the time of adversity has forgot him. His sweet charming little sensible wife, who has brought him a son since his departure, is the most unhappy of woman. I shall say no more on this subject as I am sensible everything that lies in your power will be done. I arrived the 13th instant from Africa and the West Indies in good health and high spirits and have the pleasure to tell you the merchants has given me the ship, and I shall sail again in the course of three weeks or a month as – <u>captain.</u>

I shall not have time to see my [?]relatives in the country, have not heard from them yet. When you write to Longtown[58] after receiving this, mention if you have had any opportunity of forwarding the inclosed or write Mrs. Irving. Direct to Captain Mrs. James Irving, Liverpool. I conclude my Dr. Graham wishing you every success, [...] and enjoyment in this life and am with the greatest respect your respectful humble servant.

Chr. Robson

It is universally thought here there will be no war.

Letter 34: 26th October 1790. James Irving, Dartmouth, to Mary Irving.

Dartmouth in Devonshire on board the brigg *Bacchus.*

My dearest girl,

Heaven only knows the satisfaction and pleasure I now feel in once again being at liberty and having it in my power, to address myself to from a place in England. We put in here this forenoon in want of provision, and shall sail again for London the first fair wind.[59] It is at present contrary but may shift soon.

We shall be oblidged to ride quarantine at Standgate Creek in London river for a few days, so that I shall expect to meet your letter either there or at London, directed to the care of Mr. Smith, our uncle, who will get it forwarded to me. If you knew my anxiety to hear from you, you would dispatch a cupid post haste to relieve me. I shall be on tenterhooks till I hear of your welfare, which pray heaven I may soon hear of. Should now be tolerably happy were it not for too acute a sense of our poor and dependant condition, but I trust we shall soon lift our heads and enjoy a comfortable state of mediocrity, however embarrased we may be at present. My officers are all with me, but we have many fears of being carried on board some of his Majesty's ships. How to steer clear I'm very much at a loss to invent.

Dear girl I am well assured we ly under many great and heavy obligations to our mother, and perhaps some others. At present, can only say that I entertain a just sense of them and hope soon to be able to repay them all. Kiss them all in my name. I believe they will all partake of the joy you'll feel on this occasion. My love and duty to our mother, grandmother and George most particularly and affectionately, and also to every relation and friend who you have tried during our long scene of adversity. For a little while farewell and believe me

> My dearest girl,
> Your most affectionate,
> although unfortunate husband.
> J. Irving

P.S. I am badly off with respect to cloaths, but I'll make a shift somehow or other. Let me know Mr. Dawson's sentiments with respect to me. Should transmit him the protest of self and officers, but think it more safe do it from the place where we ride quarantine.

Letter 35: 6th November 1790. James Irving at Stangate Creek, London to Mary Irving in Liverpool.

> Stangate Creek, November 6th, 1790.

Dearest girl,

I have only just time to inform you that I arrived here this morning in health, God be praised. We shall ride quarantine 4 or 5 days, and then proceed to London to discharge the cargo. In the meantime, I expect your letter on my arrival there. Have wrote to our friend Mr. Smith to endeavour to procure some sort of protection from the press gangs, as it is very hot.[60] I hope however, to escape and be blest with a happy meeting. Pardon my brevity, the quarantine boat is come alongside for the letters. Duty and love to our mother, grandmother etc. etc. Heaven bless you,

> I am,
> Dearest girl,
> Your most affectionate husband,
> J. Irving

N.B. I wrote you from Dartmouth, as also Mr. Dawson. Write for God's sake.

Most beloved wife,

I have broke open the letter to acknowledge the receipt of yours of 30th October, brought alongside by the quarantine boat. I'm unable to express my most extreme joy and happiness, and my gratitude to our benificient Creator for his bounteous mercys in keeping and preserving you and our infant in your day of trial and under the distresses that oppressed you. The Almighty will never forsake those who put their trust in him. Neither your letters, nor Uncle Anthony's nor Captain Sherwood's have I at any time received, but am most gratefull to them for their great attention to you and shall by first occasion assure them of it. Do you, however, in the meantime pay your respects to them in my name? I have received here 2 letters from good Mr. Smith, wherin he informs me that he hath procured protections for me and officers and shall send them down the moment he hears of my arrival. There is an instance of extreme benevolence. Happy should I be were it in my power to repay him. Shall trouble him for some supplys as soon as I get to London. My pride and independant spirit is considerably humbled. Misfortunes my dear Mary are unavoidable, better fortune yet awaits us. Rejoice with me and my cup will be full. My daily prayers are offered up for you, our babe, mother and grandmother, also our friends in the north and elsewhere. Again may God bless you.

J. Irving.

Have requested Mr. Smith to write Mr. Robinson (if in England), and assure him of my gratefull sense of his friendship and the attention he has showed you. Respects to Mr. Gibbins etc., etc., etc., etc., etc. You know who is who. I do [?]note you have sense and opportunity to thank our friends. I want perhaps both. Again may God bless you.

J.I.

How is brother George, you never mentioned him.

James love and respects. Put a wafer in Mrs. Sherwood's card.

Letter 36: 12th November 1790. James Irving in London to his wife, Mary, in Liverpool.

London 12th November, 1790.

My dear Mary,

It gives me much pleasure to address you from our good friend Mr. Smith's fireside, where I moored myself late last night in tolerable health with a heart as light as a lark, owing in a great measure to the pleasing accounts your letters conveyed. I have strong hopes of being with you in a few days, as I shall not stay one hour longer here than is unavoidable. Another circumstance also affords me much comfort, videlicet, the receipt of a letter from Mr. Dawson with £20 inclosed. This is a good omen, and will enable me to go to Liverpool in some degree of decency and also to assist my officers up there. My dear girl, be assured I long most ardently to be with you and <u>our little lad</u>. He may in a future day with God's blessing be a comfort to us, and conduce to render our toils and hardships supportable. Tap, rap, goes the knocker and a letter for Mr. James Irving. It is yours and our good mother's of the 12th ultimo. You see I have above anticipated the answer, shall only add that if you knew my feelings you would have no reason to inculcate haste.

Mr. Smith and I are this minute going to a cloaths shop, where I mean to get myself pretty well rigged and cast of the Arabic rags that as I thought il-fitted me. Love, duty and compliments are unnecessary. May God bless you all, prayeth fervently,

> My dear Mary,
> yours most affectiona[...],
> J. Irving.

Honoured mother,

Your natural anxiety for my welfare and your care of mine during my captivity are gratefully felt by

> Your most loving and dutyfull
> son,
> J. Irving.

X Mrs. Tunstall –

X My great grandmother, James C. Irving. [This is a note written in pencil in a different hand]

Letter 37: 2nd January 1791. James Irving II to his parents in Scotland.

> North west buoy, 6 miles fromLiverpool, January 2nd, 1791.

Honoured parents,

I duly received yours of the 21st ultimo, in answer to mine of the 17th. You said you were surprised I did not mention in my last the articles best for you to send me. The truth was I did not think you were in a condition to supply my wants. Therefore I would not write, as I knew you would straiten yourselve in order to supply me. My heart forebad me and told me not to ask what you had got by the sweat of your brows. I likewise received the bundle and everything in it safe. I also had a letter from my brother Simon.[61] He desired me to write to him before we sailed, which I have not done which I hope hee'l [?]excuse for 2 reasons. The one because I had nothing to write worth his notice, the other because ever since I received his we have been very busy loading the vessel etc. I suppose before you have read this far, you will be saying that I am gone away without telling you where I am gone to or anything else. I therefor will tell you as well as I can. We are bound for Anamaboe in the Gold Coast, discharge what goods we have for that place and set sail from it again within 48 hours after we arrived. Then we are to call at Lagus, Accra and other parts whose names I have forgot. We are then to go down as far as Benin river and stay a day or two and then go back to Anamaboe, from which place we are to sail for the West Indies.[62] My wages is £4 [?]sterling per month, besides if it please God we make a good voyage, I ~~expect to~~ get head money, and if we only bury 6 slaves my cousin will receive £100 and I £50 [?]bounty. If we bury not more than 9 slaves my couzen will receive £50 and I £25 bounty.[63] I don't expect we will be out less than 12 months, although my couzin says 10 months. However, don't let that trouble you as it makes no difference provided we keep our health, as I hope we will. I will now tell you a story in return to my brother's of the Spanish cobler. A little while ago there happened to be a gale of wind in the channel and I heard it myself reported for truth by some as respectable people as any in Liverpool that the *Globe Cutter* with 150 impressed men on board, a Scotch sloop, a vessel belonging to Liverpool and several other vessels foundered in the channel and all hands perished. This was all falsehood to the disgrace of humanity, invented by some malitious persons on purpose to make people unhappy who had any friends or relations in the vessels. You may also remember that William Nickol Taylor wrote from London about 4 years ago that my couzen was dead.[64] I mention these falsitys to put not only you, but also all the people at Langholm, upon their guard against such vague reports who has any friends or relations abroad. I will now conclude with wishing God will bless you, my brothers and other relations, which will always be the prayer of,

Honoured parents,
Your ever dutiful son,
Jas. Irving.

P.S. I was going to fill the other leaf side with compliments, but I have not time to write so you may give them as you think proper. Don't forget to tell my brother to give my compliments and sincere well wishes to William Scott, Hawick Miln.

N.B. The pilot puts this in the Liverpool post-office.   J.I.

Letter 38: 25th January 1791. James Irving anchored off present day Cumbria, to Mary Irving.

Piel Fowdrey January ye 25th, 1791.

My Mary,

As there is a prospect of a brigg sailing for Liverpool tonight, I could not neglect the opportunity to inform you that I am still here without any prospect of getting away, the wind contrary and blowing hard.[65] My spirits are but low owing to so long detention, but my health is unimpared. God grant you may be as well with our dear Jamie, mother and grandmother. Pray write me, as I'm anxious about you. Let the letter take its chance. Direct care of Mrs. Postlethwaite [...] Ulverstone, it will be sent down. You know the pleasure your letters afford, they [...] give as much now as heretofore. I know I [...] not remind you of gratitude to relations [...] other worthy friends. I had a letter from Mr. Dawson the other day. He seems anxious to have me sail, but knows it impossible. I am with all the affection you justly merit.

My Mary,
Yours unalterably,
J. Irving.

In one of mine from this place, I expressed a wish to see a copy of the policy of insurance. Send one if you can, Mr. Dawson hath not insured.

I'm very well supplied with officers, particularly the first and second mates, videlicet, Mr. Patton and Mr. Winter.[66]

Letter 39: 2nd February 1791. James Irving anchored off present day Cumbria to Mary Irving.

Ship *Ellen*, Pile Fowdrey. February 2nd, 1791.

My dearest girl,

This day yours of the 27th January was duly received. It always gives me as much comfort and delight as you can conceive to hear from you, and of your health. The indisposition of our sweet and darling little lad I confess distresseth me, yet I hope God Almighty will deal tenderly with him and we shall both be thankfull and happy. May I hope you'll not be anxious about the state of the vessel, as I have no doubt of doing well and making the voyage prosperously. Thank heavens for my being in port as the weather hath been most severe, particularly yesterday (Tuesday) when we had as violent a storm of wind as perhaps ever blew. This day the aspect of the weather is changed and I have some hope of being able to put to sea, yet I doubt it only flatters. While I am writing, it begins blowing from the north west. Pray God send a change as our anchors could scarsely hold us. I fear not my health my Mary, be not uneasy on that account.

Mr. Welsh I know and have proved to be a friend, his readiness to do that business will manifest it. Have not got a carpenter, but shall make a shift without one. Mr. Dawson I know will excuse me if I cannot fulfill his orders with respect to the boat, the *Little Devil*, I mean. As I have been so long detained and retarded contrary to my inclination, you may be assured not one single tide shall be lost and the *Ellen* shall go to sea on the least prospect of getting round Holyhead. There are 24 sail of vessels here bound to the southward and westward, and if you hear of one of them going to sea, say it is the *Ellen*. Have had some little trouble with my people, but shall tie them in spite of all their machinations. My third mate, Mr. Bailey, has proved a rascal. I watched him one night and caught him ready to get from alongside with his cloaths and two of the people. On presenting a pistol to his head, he ran and I secured him. He was shipped a stranger, although he belongs to Liverpool.

My dear girl, when you write again pray tell me what ships are sailed since I did (Guineamen are meant) and when. I think none could, if they did they must have fared worse than the *Ellen* has. Take every opportunity to call on Mr. Horriban, he will tell you all African news. Visit for once or twice Mrs. Patton, my mate's wife. He deserves that attention as a good officer and scholar, although a cooper. When you write mention her. Many kind compliments to Uncle Anthony. Hope Mr. Smith has received my narrative.[67] Many compliments to him as a worthy friend. Forget not the good lasses, his daughters. Forget not our parents in Scotland. In short, remember me to everyone who you find a true friend, the Sherwoods and Forbesses particularly, also Lintons and [?]Maxwell.[68] I am confident they are so. I presume Frank [?]Harrison hath not come to Liverpool. Shall again say fear me not. I am an old veteran in hard service and defy hardship. Had I been a coward, had been dead many years ago. Mind plenty of news and Guinea friends. I wrote to Scotland per this place [...] [...] would be [...] from me. Shall now conclude with much duty, love and respect to mother, grandmother and our most worthy brother George. I have not a friend I more value. Should you see Mr. Gibbins, offer my respects. Believe [...] constantly,

> My dear Mary,
> Yours most affectionately,
> J. Irving.

Mr. Andrew Irving's letters were missed. May send to Mr. [?]Beggs, number 7 [...] [...] and send them to me if the wind continues westerly or north west. Am sorry to go without them. February 3rd. I this moment received yours of the 28

January. Good God how undesiredly have I offended Mr. Welsh. I would sooner have forfeited my right hand than suspect him or give him a cause [...] doubt my integrity. Shall write him.

Letter 40: 14th June 1791. Captain James Irving, Africa, to his wife Mary in Liverpool.

Ellen off Benin Barr, June 14, 1791.

My dearest love,

How happy am I to say I have received your 2 kind letters by the *Princess Royal* and *Brothers* with the most welcome of all tidings, your, our parents and little Jammie good health. That the Almighty may long preserve you, so is my daily prayer. My good, nay best of girls, will be happy when she is infor[...] that I am healthy, a state I have been in since I left her. Brother George's was also received. He will yet be an honour and ornament to the family, this I propheccy, although not inspired. Remember me most affectionately to him. This line goes by the *Brothers* to be forwarded from Bonney. She is under sail going down, am therefore oblidged to cut this very short as I shall write you in two or 3 days by the *Maria*, and a very long letter. Indeed, when I sat down I meant to make this a long one, but the ship getting under weigh leaves me no time. I know my pet you'll excuse me if I conclude with love and duty to mother, grandmother and a kiss to Jamie. Gratefull respects to our friends, Sherwoods etc.

May heavens keep you till the day comes when your company and arms shall bless,

> My dearest love,
> Your ever affectionate
> husband,
> J. Irving.

J.I. and Mr. [?]Patton are both well.

LETTERS: Notes.

1. Mr. Hippins worked at the dockyard in Deptford and, on a number of occasions, arranged insurance for Irving. L.R.O., DDX 1126/34, /39.

2. *Lloyd's List* of Friday 1st December 1786 (no. 1834) recorded that 'the *Ally*, Dodson was well at New Calabar the 23rd July'.

3. Irving had served on two earlier voyages of a ship named the *Vulture* between November 1782 and May 1784. P.R.O., BT 98/43, 11th July 1783, BT 98/44, 2nd June 1784.

4. A letter from James Irving at New Calabar to his wife dated 19th July 1786 is listed in the catalogue at the L.R.O., but is now missing. L.R.O., DDX 1126/3.

5. *Lloyd's List* of Tuesday 12th December 1786 (no. 1837) records that the *Golden Age* in the command of Captain Jackson was at Bonny on the west coast of Africa.

6. Later letters indicate that this refers to his brother-in-law, George Dalston Tunstall (Letter 24).

7. This could refer to either John Marvault who died, according to details in the muster roll, on 30th August 1786 or James Maxwell who died on September 18th 1786. P.R.O., BT 98/47, 27th March 1787.

8. In the muster roll John Quirk, Hugh Christian, William Harrison, John Clegg and James Irving are listed in descending order after Captain Quayle Fargher. *Ibid.*

9. This number is broadly confirmed in *Lloyd's List* of Friday 26th January 1787 which records that the *Jane*, Fargher arrived [at Tobago] from Africa, 526 slaves'.

10. The parish registers of Langholm record the baptism of 'James son to John Irving smith in Langholm and Isobel Little his spouse' on 16th December 1759. Langholm parish registers, 1664-1854, D.A.C., MF 67.

11. Located on the west coast of Africa (see Map 3).

12. Alexander Falconbridge described Bonny as 'a large town ... lying about twelve miles from the sea on the east side of a river of the same name...'. The barr refers to a bank or shallow at the mouth of the river. Falconbridge, *Slave trade*, p. 51.

13. The muster roll lists William Baker, possibly the nephew of the merchant Peter Baker, as the final name in a crew list of 54, indicating that he was probably an apprentice. P.R.O., BT 98/48, 19th January 1788.

14. *Williamson's Liverpool Advertiser* of 7th January 1788 records that the *Garland*, W. Forbes arrived in Liverpool from Africa and Havana 'with 13 elephant teeth for Baker and Dawson'. William Forbes, baptised in Liverpool on 13th February 1753, captained six slave voyages between 1786 and 1791. Behrendt, 'Captains', p. 124.

15. The muster roll for the *Princess Royal* lists William Linton after Captain Sherwood, and John McLeish is listed eleventh after the captain. P.R.O., BT 98/48, 19th January 1788.

16. On the voyage of the *Princess Royal* between 10th April 1788 and January 22nd 1789, Robert Catterall is listed directly after Captain Sherwood. There are two people named James Irving in the list. The first, the subject of this text, is listed seventh in a total crew list of 83, whilst his younger cousin is listed two places lower. P.R.O., BT 98/49, 2nd March 1789.

17. Dialect for quilt.

18. Mrs. Tunstall was Mary Irving's mother.

19. James Irving II had three surviving brothers. The eldest, Simon, born in 1769, John, and David the youngest born in December 1778. Irving, *Scottish Poetry*, p. xi.

20. Mawlay 'Abd. al-Rahman was a son of Sidi Muhammad b. 'Abd. Allah, Emperor of Morocco between 1757 and 1790. Living in exile, he extended his political control in the remote southern territories of Morocco, including Taroudant and Goulimine, an area bordering the Sahara desert (see Map 4). El Mansour, *Morocco*, pp. 89,96.

21. This corresponds with information in Admiralty records. P.R.O., ADM 7/109, pass number 7469, ADM 7/108.

22. In the journal Irving notes in July 1789 that 'About this time I was informed by the Jew that I had been bought from Bilade at Gulimene by Sheik Brahim, my present master, for a hundred and thirty five ducats...'.

23. Mogodore (or Essaouira to use the Arabic name) is a seaport town on the Atlantic coast of Morocco, founded in 1764 by Sidi Muhammad.

24. An appeal for assistance to unnamed individuals, written by Captain Sherwood on Irving's behalf, survives in the L.C.R.O., 387 MD 28 (Letter 30).

25. This is probably an error in transcription by John Hutchison (or his clerk) as the address on surviving letters between 1789 and 1791 is 7 Pownall Square, Liverpool. L.R.O., DDX 1126/10, /13, /20, /25, /30, /31, /33, /35, /36.

26. Mawlay 'Abd. al-Salam son of Sidi Muhammad, Emperor of Morocco, was virtually blind.

27. In a letter to the Secretary of State's office dated 17th August 1789, Matra noted that 'Muly Islemma has already purchased two of Captain Irving's crew who are now with Muly Abdslem at Morocco...' P.R.O., FO 52/8, 119.

28. Aaron Debauny, the Jew with whom Irving was housed (Letter 20).

29. The register of Mediterranean Passes shows that the pass was returned on 24th August 1789. P.R.O., ADM 7/109, ADM 7/108.

30. Mary Irving gave birth to a son James on 4th December 1789. L.C.R.O., MF 1/32, RG 4/1042.

31. John Irving of Langholm in Scotland died in 1807, aged 76. D.A.C., *Memorials of Langholm Parish*, reference 18.

32. Benin City, or Great Benin, was some miles inland from the coast. Although Irving, like many other sailors, referred to 'Benin', the city, located well inland, was not accessible to ships (see Map 3).

33. This corresponds with information in the journal, in which Irving records in July 1789, 'received a letter from my officers and people, in which they complained pitifully of the usage they received'.

34. Matthew Dawson, the second mate, was a nephew of John Dawson, the owner of the *Anna*, and one of the world's leading slave traders. The apprentice was named Samuel Beeley (Letter 10). See note 27 above.

35. In a letter dated 27th September 1789, Matra acknowledged receipt of a letter from Irving dated 10th August (Letter 21). The collection in the L.R.O. includes a draft of a letter to Matra in an extremely fragile condition. In this letter, Irving writes 'I am a most distresst and unfortunate person takes the liberty of addressing you and craves with the humility of a poor slave your assistance and protection...'. L.R.O., DDX 1126/16.

36. His name is variously spelt as Atall and Attar. In a letter to the Secretary of State's office dated 4th December 1789, Matra describes Atall as 'the Emperor's favourite Jew and the man who since my last journey to court has chiefly managed for me there in private...' In the same letter Matra reported that 'Having others employed at court by this time, I have limited Atall's business solely to procuring me the seamen, which with great confidence he says he shall accomplish'. P.R.O., FO 52/8, 173.

37. A governor of a town. Lempriere, *Tour*, p. 17.

38. This may well have been based on the draft letter in the L.R.O. Although the letter is not dated, Irving explains to Matra that he first established contact with Hutchison six weeks previously. As the surviving copies of these letters amongst consular papers are dated 24th and 25th June, this suggests that the draft letter to Matra was composed early to mid August 1789. See note 35 above. L.R.O., DDX 1126/16.

39. The doctor, William Lempriere, wrote a detailed account of his experiences in Morocco between September 1789 and February 1790. Lempriere, *Tour, passim.*

40. In his journal Irving describes how 'Early in September I experienced another attack of fever, which rendered me delirious during the hot stage of the paroxism which seized me everyday. I wrote to Mogodore for medicine and received some, which was all the Consul could procure of what I wanted'.

41. In the journal Irving records that in August 1789 William Brown, John Richards and Jack Peters were purchased by his master Sheik Brahim and transferred to 'Telling'. He also records that early in October 1789 the same three men were 'redeemed and taken away by some officers of the Emperor'.

42. This refers to John Clegg, the first mate, Joseph Pearson, a seaman, and Silvin Buckle one of the three 'Portuguese blacks' (Letter 10).

43. Taroudant was the usual residence of his intended patient, Mawlay 'Abd. al-Salam. In his *Tour* Lempriere records that he reached Taroudant on 28th October 1789. Lempriere, *Tour*, pp. 120-171.

44. This brief account can be compared with the more detailed account in Irving's journal.

45. A substitute.

46. Jackson noted that Mr. A. Layton was a British merchant at Mogodore and the 'chief partner in a house of considerable capital and respectability'. He is mentioned frequently in Matra's correspondence. Jackson, *Morocco*, 263-5; see for example P.R.O., FO 52/8, 152.

47. In his *Tour* Lempriere described how he enjoyed Irving's company at Morocco (Marrakech) in January 1790. Lempriere experienced some difficulty in obtaining the Emperor's permission to return to the garrison in Gibraltar. Lempriere, *Tour*, p. 274 ff.

48. In the journal Irving records that the crew of the *Anna* left the city of Morocco (Marrakech) on January 18th 1790 and arrived at Mogodore three days later.

49. The first letter which Matra wrote to the Secretary of State's office concerning the crew of the *Anna* is dated 21st July 1789 (Letter 13). Matra makes frequent reference to the men in subsequent letters. P.R.O., FO 52/8, 105ff.

50. His cousin and namesake was aged 17 or 18. D.A.C., *Memorials of Langholm Parish*, reference 5.

51. This is consistent with information contained in letters from Matra to the Secretary of State's office dated 22nd and 27th March 1790. P.R.O., FO 52/8, 199-201.

52. In the journal Irving records that James Drachen, a 'Portuguese black', died at 'Telling' in October 1789. A report later written by Matra confirms that it was James Drachen who died in captivity as his is the only name missing from a crew list that the Consul General sent to Whitehall in December 1789. P.R.O., FO 52/8, 177-180.

53. Liverpool muster rolls reveal that between April 1787 and January 1789, Irving sailed to Africa and Havana on two voyages of the *Princess Royal* in the command of Sherwood. P.R.O., BT 98/48, 19th January 1788; BT 98/49, 2nd March 1789.

54. Pwllheli on Cardigan Bay, North Wales .

55. Irving was aware he would need to renew his certificate before he could undertake any further voyages. See journal, note 28.

56. A buff coloured cotton cloth.

57. Langholm is situated on the banks of the River Esk.

58. Longtown is situated between Carlisle and Langholm.

59. *Lloyd's List* of Tuesday 9th November 1790 recorded that the *Bacchus*, Prouting had arrived at Stangate Creek.

60. Hugh Crow referred to being 'apprehensive of being impressed' in August 1790 as 'we learned from a brig of war that England was on the eve of going to war with Spain'. Crow, *Memoirs*, p. 31.

61. Simon, the eldest son of Janetus and Helen Irving, established himself as a successful merchant in London. Irving, *Scottish Poetry*, p. xi.

62. The pattern of the voyage he describes is consistent with information contained in the 'Return to an Order of the Right Honourable the House of Lords dated 10th July 1799' in which the Clerk of the Parliament had been directed to extract several categories of information from the 'several log books and journals of ships employed in the slave trade in each year from 1791 to 1797...'. H.L.R.O., HL Main Papers, 28th July 1800.

63. Clause XIV of the Dolben Act of 1788 stated that £100 should be paid to the master and £50 to the surgeon if 'there shall not have died more than in the proportion of two slaves in the hundred, from the time of the arrival of such ship or vessel on the coast of Africa, to the time of her arrival at her port of discharge in any of the islands in the West Indies...' A bounty of £50 for the master and £25 for the surgeon was payable if 'there shall not have died more than in the proportion of three slaves in the hundred...'. An Act to regulate for a limited time, the shipping and carrying of slaves in British vessels from the coast of Africa', Donnan, *History of the slave trade,* p. 587.

64. Four years previously James Irving was on board the *Jane* in the command of Quayle Fargher and was then entered on board the *Princess Royal* with Captain Sherwood for a voyage to Africa and Havana in April 1787. The reason for this observation though is unclear. P.R.O., BT 98/47, 27th March 1787, BT 98/48, 19th January 1788.

65. The Pile of Fouldrey is a channel located to the south-west of Ulverston in Cumbria.

66. Thomas Patton and Joseph Winters are listed after Captain Irving in the muster roll. P.R.O., BT 98/52, 31st July 1792.

67. This reference could indicate that James Irving sent a copy of his journal to his uncle in London. The copy in the L.R.O. suggests that the original from which it was

transcribed was 'wrote by Mr. Irving for his much loved brother-in-law, George Dalston Tunstall'. L.R.O., DDX 1126/1.
68. He clearly regarded William Sherwood and William Forbes, Liverpool slave captains, as personal friends.

Bibliography

PRIMARY SOURCES

Manuscript:

Public Record Office (P.R.O.)
'An account of all vessels which have cleared for London, Bristol and Liverpool to Africa since the year 1788', T64/286.
Liverpool Muster Rolls, 1782-1792, BT 98/42-52.
Register of Mediterranean passes, 1787-1790, ADM 7/108, ADM 7/109.
Correspondence of James M. Matra, 1789-90, FO 52/8.
Various papers of James M. Matra, 1772-1792, FO 52/9.
Miscellaneous, including legal documents and accounts of ransom paid and presents bought for the Sultan, FO 174/2.
General correspondence, 1785-1806, FO 174/284.
From the Ironmongers' Company, London, regarding the redemption of British slaves and shipwrecked mariners in Morocco, FO 174/14.

House of Lords Record Office (H.L.R.O.)
Petitions of John Dawson, merchant of Liverpool, H.L. Main Papers, 3rd July and 10th July, 1788.
'Return ... of ships employed in the slave trade in each year from 1791 to 1797...',
H.L. Main Papers, 28th July 1800.
Extracts from the log and journal of the '*Ellen* of Liverpool', H.L. Main Papers, 28th June, 1799.

Dumfries Archive Centre (D.A.C.)
Langholm parish registers, 1668-1854, MF 67.

Lancashire Record Office (L.R.O.)
Copy of James Irving's journal, 1789-90, DDX 1126/1.
Correspondence relating to James Irving, 1789-1809, DDX 1126/2-45.

Liverpool City Record Office (L.C.R.O.)
Register of births and baptisms belonging to the Congregation of Protestant Dissenters at Benns Garden Chapel, 1734-1832, MF 1/32.
Register of certificates granted to ... surgeons of the African trade, 614 INF 9/1.
Letter from Captain William Sherwood to unnamed individuals, 387 MD 28.

Merseyside Maritime Museum Archive (M.M.M.A.)
Customs Registers of Shipping, C/EX/L/4, vols. 4-8.
Atlas of Charts, 1794, OA 1866.

Printed Sources.

Newspapers:
Lloyd's List, 1781 & 1782 (Farnborough, 1969).
Lloyd's List, 1783 & 1784 (Farnborough, 1969).
Lloyd's List, 1785 & 1786 (Farnborough, 1969).
Lloyd's List, 1787 & 1788 (Farnborough, 1969).
Lloyd's List, 1789 & 1790 (Farnborough, 1969).
Lloyd's List, 1791 & 1792 (Farnborough, 1969).
Williamson's Liverpool Advertiser, 1787 - 1792.

Books:
Aspinall, A., ed., *The correspondence of George Prince of Wales*, vol. II (London, 1964).
Crow, Hugh, *Memoirs of the late Captain Hugh Crow of Liverpool* (London, 1970).
Donnan, Elizabeth, ed., *Documents illustrative of the history of the slave trade to America*, vol. II (Washington, 1931).
Enfield, William, *An essay towards the history of Liverpool* (Warrington, 1773).
Falconbridge, Alexander, *An account of the slave trade on the coast of Africa* (London, 1788).
A Genuine "Dicky Sam", *Liverpool and slavery: an historical account of the Liverpool-African slave trade* (Liverpool 1884, reprinted 1985).
Jackson, James Grey, *An account of the Empire of Morocco*, 3rd edition (London, 1968).
Lempriere, William, *A tour from Gibraltar to Tangier, Sallee, Mogodore, Santa Cruz, Tarudant, and thence over Mount Atlas to Morocco*, 3rd edition (London, 1804).
Martin, Bernard and Spurrell, Mark, ed., *The journal of a slave trader (John Newton) 1750-1754* (London, 1962).

Martin, Eveline, ed., *Journal of a slave dealer* (London, 1930).
Memorials of Langholm Parish, reference work held at D.A.C.
The New Statistical Account of Scotland, vol. iv. Dumfries-Kircudbright-Wigston (London, 1845).

SECONDARY SOURCES.

Anstey, Roger, *The Atlantic slave trade and British abolition, 1760-1810* (London, 1975).
Anstey, Roger and Hair, P.E.H., ed., *Liverpool, the African slave trade and abolition*, Historic Society of Lancashire and Cheshire, Occasional series, vol. 2 (1989).
Behrendt, Stephen D., 'The captains in the British slave trade from 1785 to 1807', *T.H.S.L.C.,* vol. 140 (1991), pp. 79-140.
Bennett, N.R., 'Christian and Negro slaves in eighteenth century North Africa', *J.A.H.*, vol. i (1960), pp. 65-82.
Bolt, Christine and Drescher, Seymour, ed., *Anti-slavery, religion and reform: essays in memory of Roger Anstey* (Folkestone, 1980).
Boog Watson, W.N., 'The Guinea trade and some of its surgeons', *Journal of the Royal College of Surgeons of Edinburgh*, vol. xiv, no. 4 (July 1969), pp. 203-214.
Clark, G.N., Crump, C.G., Jenkins, C., Jenkinson, H., Little, A.G., Poole, R.L. and Notestein, W., 'Principles for the construction of a printed text', *Bulletin of the Institute of Historical Research*, vol. i (1923-25), pp. 6-25.
Cohn, Raymond L., 'Discussion: mortality in the French slave trade', *J.A.H.*, vol. 23 (1982), pp. 225-226.
Curtin, Philip D., *The Atlantic slave trade: a census* (Madison, 1969).
Drescher, Seymour, 'The slaving capital of the world: Liverpool and national opinion in the age of abolition', *Slavery and Abolition*, vol. 9, no. 2 (September 1988), pp. 128-143.
Dunn, Richard S., ' "Dreadfull idlers" in the cane fields: the slave labor pattern on a Jamaican sugar estate, 1762-1831', *J.I.H.,* vol. xvii, no. 4 (Spring 1987), pp. 795-822.
El Mansour, Mohamed, *Morocco in the reign of Mawlay Sulayman* (Wisbech, 1990).
Engerman, Stanley L. and Genovese, Eugene D., ed., *Race and slavery in the Western Hemisphere: quantitative studies* (Princeton, 1975).
Flint, John E., ed., *The Cambridge History of Africa*, vol. 5 (Cambridge, 1976).
Gemery, H.A. and Hogendorn, Jan S. ed., *The Uncommon Market: essays in the economic history of the Atlantic slave trade* (New York, 1979).

Gray, Richard, ed., *The Cambridge History of Africa*, vol. 4 (Cambridge, 1975).

Hair, P.E.H., *The Atlantic slave trade and Black Africa* (The Historical Association, 1978).

Hair, P.E.H., 'Antera Duke of Old Calabar - a little more about an African entrepreneur', *H.A.*, vol. 17 (1990), pp. 359-65.

Inikori, J.E., 'Measuring the Atlantic slave trade: an assessment of Curtin and Anstey', *J.A.H.*, vol. xvii, no. 2 (1976), pp. 197-223.

Inikori, Joseph E. and Engerman, Stanley Lewis, ed., *The Atlantic slave trade: effects on economies, societies and peoples in Africa, the Americas and Europe* (London, 1992).

Irving, David, *The History of Scottish Poetry* (Edinburgh, 1861).

Karras, Alan L., 'Of human bondage: creating an Atlantic history of slavery', *J.I.H.*, vol. xxii, no. 2 (Autumn 1991), pp. 285-293.

Leech, William B., 'Notes on a visit to Mogador', *Journal of the Manchester Geographical Society*, vol. 18 (1905), pp. 57-64.

Liverpool Nautical Research Society, *Liverpool shipbuilders and the ships they built* (Unpublished reference work kept at M.M.M.A.).

Lovejoy, Paul E., 'The volume of the Atlantic slave trade: a synthesis', *J.A.H.*, vol. 23 (1982), pp. 473-501.

Lovejoy, Paul E., *Transformations in slavery: a history of slavery in Africa* (Cambridge, 1983).

Manning, Patrick, *Slavery and African life: occidental, oriental and African slave trades* (Cambridge, 1990).

Minchinton, Walter E., 'Characteristics of British slaving vessels, 1698-1775', *J.I.H.*,, vol. xx, no. 1 (Summer, 1989), pp. 53-81.

Rézette, Robert, *The western Sahara and the frontiers of Morocco* (Paris, 1975).

Richardson, David ed., *Abolition and its aftermath: the historical context 1790-1916* (London, 1985).

Richardson, David ed., *Bristol, Africa and the eighteenth century slave trade to America, vol. 1. The years of expansion, 1698-1729*, Bristol Record Society Publications, vol. xxxviii (1986).

Richardson, David ed., *Bristol, Africa and the eighteenth century slave trade to America, vol. 2. The years of ascendancy, 1730-45*, Bristol Record Society Publications, vol. xxxix (1987).

Richardson, David, 'The costs of survival: the transport of slaves in the Middle Passage and the profitability of the 18th century British slave trade', *E.E.H.*, vol. 24 (1987), pp. 178-196.

Richardson, David, 'The slave trade, sugar and British economic growth, 1748-1776', *J.I.H.*, vol. xvii, no. 4 (Spring 1987), pp. 739-769.

Richardson, D., 'Slave exports from West and West Central Africa, 1700-1810:

new estimate of volume and distribution', *J.A.H.*, vol. 30 (1989), pp. 1-22.

Richardson, David ed., *Bristol, Africa and the eighteenth century slave trade to America, vol. 3. The years of decline, 1746-69*, Bristol Record Society Publications, vol. xlii (1991).

Sanderson, F.E., 'The Liverpool delegates and Sir William Dolben's Bill', *T.H.S.L.C.*, vol. 124 (1972), pp. 57-84.

Schofield, M.M., 'The slave trade from Lancashire and Cheshire ports outside Liverpool, c. 1750-c.1790', *T.H.S.L.C.*, vol. 126 (1977), pp. 30-72.

Schroeter, D.J., 'Merchants and pedlars of Essaouira: a social history of a Moroccan trading town, 1844-1884' (Unpublished Ph.D thesis, University of Manchester, 1984).

Stein, Robert, 'Mortality in the eighteenth century French slave trade', *J.A.H.*, vol. 21 (1980), pp. 35-41.

Tibbles, Anthony ed., *Transatlantic slavery: against human dignity* (London, 1994).

Truckell, A.E., 'Some 18th century transatlantic trade documents', unpublished article, a copy of which is deposited in the D.A.C.

Wallis, P.J. & R.V., *Eighteenth century medics*, 2nd edition (Newcastle upon Tyne, 1988).

Williams, G., *History of the Liverpool privateers and letters of marque with an account of the Liverpool slave trade* (London, 1897).

INDEX

Where known, modern spellings of personal and place names are adopted. Contemporary spellings and alternative spellings are listed in brackets where they are significantly different from the modern form. Where the modern equivalent is not known, the most common spelling is listed.

Names

Places